SOMERSET BIRDS AND SOME OTHER FOLK

SOMERSET BIRDS

AND SOME OTHER FOLK

by

E. W. HENDY

with an Introduction by

H. J. MASSINGHAM

1944

EYRE & SPOTTISWOODE

LONDON

Opposite : Snow on Dunkery
May 17th 1935

First published December 1943
Reprinted February 1944

BOOK
PRODUCTION
WAR ECONOMY
STANDARD

Printed in Great Britain
for Eyre & Spottiswoode (Publishers), Ltd.
15 Bedford Street, Strand, London, W.C.2

FOREWORD

This book, like *Wild Exmoor Through the Year*, has a West Country setting. It tells of my experiences with the birds of Exmoor and the Somerset countryside but also has something to say about other country creatures, human and unhuman. I have made an intensive study of chaffinches and robins and to a less extent of other common species which haunt our gardens. These biographies show how ignorant we are of the life histories of some of our everyday birds and how much of interest still remains to be discovered by constant and patient watching. This aspect of bird study has so far been neglected or overlooked; more attention has been paid by writers and photographers to the rarer species. This is all to the good, but it should not be allowed to blind us to the fascination of observing and becoming intimate with what is near at hand. I hope what I have written may stimulate others to make investigations on similar lines. The chapter on merlins and the observations on ravens (in Chapter XVII) are also the result of watching, over some eighteen years, birds which are uncommon except in certain localities. I also discuss, under 'Bird Problems', the question of birds pairing for life, and bird behaviour, a subject still little understood. The facts mentioned, and illustrated, about the position of the woodcock's ear are not commonly known or appreciated even by shooting men. And, greatly daring, I have tried to review impartially the vexed question whether the adder swallows her young.

Perhaps an apology is due for the introduction of a few short pieces of verse. Or perhaps not.

E. W. H.

PORLOCK, *January,* 1943

CONTENTS

CHAPTER   PAGE

INTRODUCTION BY H. J. MASSINGHAM - - - 9

THE DUNNOCK'S NEST (*Verse*) - - - - 12

I. AN EXMOOR GARDEN AND ITS BIRDS - - - 13

II. 'SMALL DEER' ON EXMOOR - - - - - 20

III. MERLINS ON EXMOOR - - - - - - 29

IV. SPRING MIGRATION OF SWALLOWS IN SOUTH WEST ENGLAND - - - - - - - - 37

V. TALES OF AN EXMOOR VILLAGE - - - - 44

VI. 'CONSIDER THE CHAFFINCH' - - - - - 51

VII. THE CHAFFINCH FURTHER CONSIDERED - - - 59

VIII. OUR TAME CHAFFINCHES - - - - - 67

IX. A MENDIP WOODMAN - - - - - - 76

X. BIRD BEHAVIOUR: ROUTINE AND INTELLIGENCE - 84

XI. SOME BIRD PROBLEMS - - - - - - 92

XII. SOME BIRD BIOGRAPHIES - - - - - 100

XIII. BIRDS AND LANDSCAPES - - - - - 109

XIV. THE QUANTOCKS - - - - - - - 117

XV. BLACKCOCK AND BLUEBELLS ON EXMOOR - - 121

XVI. PORLOCK MARSH - - - - - - 125

XVII. EXCITEMENTS OF AN EXMOOR BIRDWATCHER - - 130

XVIII. THE KINDLY INFLUENCE OF BIRDS - - - 139

XIX. AUTUMN BIRD-SONG - - - - - - 144

XX. DOES THE ADDER SWALLOW HER YOUNG? - - 148

XXI. MOORLAND PEACE - - - - - - 154

RETURN (*Verse*) - - - - - - 158

LIST OF ILLUSTRATIONS

Snow on Dunkery, May 17th 1935, *photograph by the author* - - - - - - - - *Frontispiece*

Plate

1. Hedgehog and female adder with young, *photographs, Col. H. Morrey Salmon, M.C.* - - - *facing page* 16

2. Wood-warbler at nest, *photographs, J. H. Sears* - - 17

3. The Porlock that is past, *photograph, Alfred Vowles* - 32

4. Another view of Old Porlock, *photograph, Alfred Vowles* 33

5. Cock chaffinch at nest, *photograph, Frances Pitt* - - 64

6. Young merlins partly fledged. Chaffinch's nest built on the top of a wren's nest, *photographs by the author* - - 65

7. Nuthatch, *photographs, J. H. Sears* - - - - - 80

8. Young cuckoo, *photograph, Frances Pitt* - - - 81

9. Cock stonechat, *photograph, J. H. Sears* - - - - 96

10. Hen stonechat, *photograph, J. H. Sears* - - - - 97

11. Greenshank in act of sitting down on her nest. Spotted flycatcher, *photographs, Frances Pitt* - - - - 112

12. Woodlark at nest, *photograph, J. H. Sears* - - - 113

13. Fledged young ravens in nest, *photograph, J. H. Sears* - 128

14. Young ravens, a few days old, in nest. Young ravens, close-up of gape. Raven's nest and eggs, *photographs, J. H. Sears* - - - - - - - - 129

Note.—All the illustrations are copyright and are reproduced by permission of the owners whose names are given.

INTRODUCTION

It is quite a long time ago since my epistolary friendship with the author of this volume began, and now the opportunity presents itself of putting on record some part of the rather complex sentiments the contents of his long letters (a number of them in expanded and tidier form appear in the book) aroused in me. The arrival of a letter from Hendy was always an event. What new rarity had he seen this time on Exmoor or Porlock Marsh (I shall never forget his maddeningly dramatic letter about the Cream-Coloured Courser whose identity he kept cunningly concealed up to p. 4, gradually heightening the tension)? What new amazing bird had nested in his macrocarpa hedge? What new instalment in the *chroniques scandaleuses* of the matrimonial irregularities of his robins had he to disclose? The first few pages of this book will give the reader some notion of the sensationalism of his letters. For in the most casual manner he relates how a kestrel killed a blue tit in his bird-bath and a magpie ate a slow-worm on the garden path; how woodlarks nested within forty yards of his window and cirl buntings in his hedge; how a hen nightingale sipped from that same bird-bath and grey wagtails, long-tailed tits and a black redstart came on or about the lawn within a few minutes of one another. But these visitations to this Hesperidean garden of his (who but Hendy has ever had a woodcock feeding on his lawn?) were not half of the tale those surprising letters of his unfolded. What magic was in the man when our commoner birds that to us, so much less gifted in observation or magnetism, appear to perform no more than their wonted routines, to him revealed such an unveiling of intimacies, such individual unexpectedness and indeed eccentricities of behaviour? What power was in him that his garden birds put aside their justly acquired suspicions and accepted him as once his feathered companions accepted Adam in another garden?

The consequence was that through his letters Hendy's garden became a bright legend in my mind. I have a garden almost as large as his but how ordinary and everydayish are my encounters with and adventures among birds compared with his! So, with something of awe, much wonder, profound appreciation of these vicarious pleasures he afforded me, not a little amusement, a spice of envy and a certain nostalgia when I considered that my bird-watching days are now a memory, I came to regard him as something of a magician who possessed a passport to what he calls 'the multicoloured minds' of birds to which we commoners are strangers. I thought of his garden, whose one horizon is the heights of Exmoor and the other the Black Mountains, as a kind of paradisal speck in our so injured and insulted land, and indeed, when he related some incident in the biographies of his feathered familiars which reflected a rather steeper decline from marital virtue than usual, as a garden of Boccaccio or one of those gardens in Burton's Arabian Nights or of the Mogul Emperors, wherein such deviations have a touch of enchantment too mythical for criticism.

Those letters have now become a solid book containing their charms and surprises and going far beyond them. And the achievement of the book is that the emotional pitch excited in me by the letters has not been dissipated by the more general and objective appeal of book-form. But because it is a book, I must no longer yield to those epistolary beguilements from which part of the book took shape. From a subjective surrender I have to school myself to an analytic scrutiny. What is the peculiar quality of Hendy the naturalist that makes his detailed and sometimes minute observations of his native birds and squirrels and stoats and others, not to exclude his gracious memorial of the woodman who married his nurse, like a fairy tale not of fancy but of fact? I think it is this. These particularities of his, so full of novelty and discovery, are that very rare thing, a true modernism that has developed out of the subconscious memory of us islanders who once loved our native land. This development has nothing whatever to do with progress; it is in fact the reverse of it because progress, by regarding the past as 'obsolete', is an idealisation of loss of memory. But Hendy has not forgotten that ancient love of our island which so many fond annalists of our island scene have painted, whether in words or from the palette or in the music-book, from St. Columba and St. Cuthbert through the illuminated manuscripts of the 14th century to Surrey and Wyatt, and on through Shakespeare and the song-books to George Herbert and Jeremy Taylor, and on again from Evelyn and Cowley to Gilbert White, Thomson, Collins and the water-colourists up to the begetters of the 'Lyrical Ballads', to John Clare and Miss Mitford and Keats as far as Bridges, Barnes and Hudson, a motley, a nondescript company but all celebrants of our pearl of great price set in the western ocean. All these figures and many more, together with the anonymous builders of our villages and little towns and the husbandmen who turned wild into domestic England without robbing her of her inborn graces, all these have left as their legacy the English tradition, and this our Hendy inherits, to this is he faithful.

But to this noble heritage which he expresses by his attitude to the creatures of his home and their landscape, in his hatred of a fragmented pseudo-science and in his natural philosophy, he adds something new. That is investigation into the inward lives and domestic affairs of the creatures of his book. Gilbert White, of course, blazed the trail, but a great deal of what Hendy reveals both of avian pattern and individuality would have astonished even the father of all our bird-watchers. Thus Hendy shows us the immeasurable flexibility of that tradition which so many busybodies and dryasdusts and Utopians and money-changers and office-holders 'drest in a little brief authority' are in our own times bent upon destroying. In his own field he may be said to have removed from science those blinkers which its own specialism and systematisation have clapped upon it, so that it may take a look all round instead of so foolishly and arrogantly mistaking the part for the whole. In a word, he has truly interpreted the meaning of the word 'vision' which means seeing with a dual sight, with the external eye but also with the inward or pineal eye which in scientific orthodoxy has become atrophied.

H. J. MASSINGHAM

THE DUNNOCK'S NEST

There, in the tangled bit of hedge
Along our apple orchard's edge,
A sly slim dunnock built her nest,
Shaping it smooth with bill and breast;
And you can see, if you peep through,
Four eggs of deepest, purest blue,
Caerulean tinct of sky or sea:
They thrilled me through with ecstasy
Keen as when first, in Asham Wood,
A child, in wonder wrapt, I stood,
And saw amid a holly's shield,
Their perfect loveliness revealed.

God, when I cease to feel the thrill
Of Beauty fire my sense, and fill
Body and soul with fine delight
In glory born of sound or sight—
Harmonious viols featly played,
Cliffs that decline to depths of jade,
Buzzards a-sail on taut, still wings,
Goldfinches' raindrop twitterings—
Oh then, in mercy, God, I pray
Give to my senses swift decay;
His heart, whom Beauty thrills no more
Like ill-stored fruit rots at its core.

CHAPTER I

AN EXMOOR GARDEN AND ITS BIRDS

When, some twenty years ago, we decided to come and live at Porlock, my wife and I found the selection of a plot of land upon which to build a difficult business. We wished to be in the country but yet not too isolated: to face our house southwards so as to have a place in the sun and a view of the distant moor, but yet not to live so close to hills that they would oppress and overshadow us.

In the end we chose a piece of land east of Porlock about one hundred and sixty feet above sea level. Viewing it from various altitudes and at all times of day we found that it held the sun longer than any other field thereabouts.

A house built there would look southwards over pasture and woodland rising gradually to where the bulk of Robin Howe, brindled in winter with ling and faded fern, slopes gently from the east for a mile and more to the twin cairns on its summit. Nearer was the rounded hillock called Crawter, an outpost of Exmoor; eastward you saw the woods of Selworthy, the hump of Bossington Beacon; northwards lay the rocky hog's back which ends in Hurlstone Point, and across the Bristol Channel in clear weather rose the cliffs of Glamorgan and the dim outlines of Welsh mountains. On the west the land was sheltered from the prevailing wind by a straggling copse.

In building our house we hoped to construct something that was not obtrusive. For that reason we chose the local red stone and brown sandfaced tiles, and with apparent success, for a neighbour whose windows looked across the valley to ours exclaimed: 'I like your house: I can't see it!' Very subtle flattery! And certainly it seemed to merge pleasantly in the red earth of Porlock Vale and the russet winter tints of Crawter.

When first we saw our one-acre-and-a-third plot staked out—a stony wilderness of ploughed field—we thought we should never fill up all that space. But as the house gradually rose, stone by stone, and the garden took shape, our feelings changed. It is wonderful how even a few small, naked trees break up space and reduce large patches of bare ground to reasonable proportions. To plan out your land increases your sense of possession, and to plant trees in it sets the final seal of ownership; you take root at the same time as they.

13

Certainly we need have had no fears about the empty spaces. The luxuriance of the Porlock soil and climate saw to that. Our hedges of *cupressus macrocarpa* on two sides of the lawn were ten feet high in six years: now they are four feet thick: cirl buntings love them as nesting places. Later on we acquired a strip of wild ground, to the south, and planted along its boundary fence alternate rowans and birches (it was Dorothy Wordsworth who described a birch as 'like a spirit of water'), and in one corner larches, spindle, and hazel bushes, as a screen against any red-brick and asbestos eruption which an unknown future may hold for us. Up and down this strip we have scattered primroses, daffodils and narcissi, and they have spread in constellations all along the hedgerow on both sides. Sweet violets, too, we planted there, and after some six years they crept quietly along the hedge-bottom and peeped at us from among their sheltering leaves. Here and there are an early purple orchid, a chequered fritillary ('mother-uglies' is a Somerset name for them), and clumps of bluebells. It is at once the most untidy and most natural part of our garden. In the hedge bounding the lane are a tall elm and a fairly large oak.

Digging operations in what eventually became our kitchen garden produced a copper coin which proved to be one of 'Drapier's pence', or 'Wood's halfpence'. The story of this coinage is historical. A patent had been acquired by one William Wood for supplying Ireland with copper halfpence, the profit on the transaction to be divided between Wood and George I's favourite, the Duchess of Kendal. Swift attacked the transaction in six famous letters written by him in 1724 under the pseudonym 'M. B. Drapier'. As a result the patent was cancelled; but Wood was rather surprisingly given a pension; Swift's popularity in Ireland rose to a very high level. Ireland was badly in need of small currency, but the scandal lay in the manner of the division of the profit, i.e. difference between the intrinsic and nominal value of the coins, which at the present day would belong to the National Treasury; and, further, the transaction was arranged without consulting and against the will of the Irish representatives. It would be interesting to know how this coin reached a Porlock field. I have heard that the halfpence were minted at Bristol. Perhaps it dropped from the pack of some moorland pony.

It was a delightful surprise to find that our land was haunted by woodlarks. We had seen and heard them before in the Exmoor district, but they were still something of a mystery to us, a 'wandering voice', like Wordsworth's cuckoo. Imagine, then, our pleasure when in our very first spring they chose to nest in the rough grass only forty yards from our windows. They were, indeed, 'good companions' to us for ten years, and nested half-a-dozen times within our boundaries. Their courtship, their song—so ethereal in quality that they seem more sprite than bird—their nesting and family cares, all became intimately known to us. The histories of some of these pairs I have set down in *The Lure of Bird Watching*. But, alas, they have now deserted us; it is three years since I have heard one sing over our garden. The sprites have faded into thin air.

Being bird lovers we set out to make our garden attractive to birds. Bird-tables and baths, and nesting boxes were among its first furnishings. The birds soon found by experience that our garden was a sanctuary with a regular food supply. In cold weather, while our land is thronged with starvelings in feathers, I have often found the grounds of a neighbouring house, which is often uninhabited, almost denuded of bird-life.

One of our bird-tables is just outside our windows. It affords an ideal opportunity to learn the table-manners of birds. Their variety is infinite.

When breakfast is spread on lawn and table a swarm of small hungry people descends to feed. Blue and great tits squabble with each other on the table, but the cole and the marsh tits snatch a crumb and depart to devour it in solitude; greenfinches plop down solidly upon the board and feed purposefully, quarrelling sometimes among themselves but not heeding the other guests; chaffinches are more volatile: some hiss at and bully an intruder: others allow themselves to be ejected even by smaller birds. The pied wagtail flutters down from the roof to the table like a shuttlecock, jigetting his tail up and down as he pecks; but his visits are short: he prefers the green table-cloth of the lawn. Robins arrive with nerves all on edge; they bounce up and down like small red and green rubber balls and bolt their beakfuls. One of them is the sworn enemy of a dunnock whom he will not allow on the table. But robins do not stay long; they prefer to return later when the rush is over and they can breakfast in peace. Sparrows have no manners: they thrust and shove and elbow their way through the crowd and no one, not even the gawky, rather stupid-looking song-thrush, can turn them off. They are the only guests which are not welcome. Starlings are eager and pushful: they gobble up everything greedily. Rarer visitors were a siskin, a blackcap and a whitethroat.

A wild bird objects to a human being looking it in the face; in fact in the field few wait long enough to give the observer the chance. Some, even when they become comparatively tame on the bird table or at other places where food is supplied artificially, never get over this reluctance. One or two tame blue tits will feed on a suspended piece of fat while I am only a couple of yards away. If I refrain my eyes from looking into theirs they are temporarily re-assured, but as soon as our eyes meet they wilt under the strain and depart in a panic. My tame chaffinches and greenfinches look up into my face fearlessly and so does one thrush. A very domesticated robin used to stare us out of countenance till we produced the expected sultana: but if you want to tame a semi-wild bird and lead it to learn confidence in you it is a good rule never to look it in the face.

A bird-bath, placed near our windows, has given us many delight-ful bird-pictures. Birds, like humans, are impatient of one individual taking too much time in the bathroom. It was a pleasant sight one morning to see a willow-warbler bathe: at close quarters it is such a slim, delicate birdling. It was ousted by a cock cirl bunting that wanted a drink, and retired to adjacent rose-bushes to dry itself. When the cirl bunting had finished the willow-warbler returned for a second dip.

Cirl buntings are very fond of bathing: you would expect so tidy a little bird to be cleanly; I have seen a hen of this species make a most thorough toilet and remain in the water for quite five minutes.

The wren's method of bathing is individualistic: one day while we were at tea a wren flew across the lawn and scurried to the edge of our shallow bird-bath: at first he stood on the margin and flicked a few drops over his head and shoulders, but although he dipped his bill into the water he shirked putting his head under. Then he backed into the bath, an original method of entering it, but appar-ently usual, for I have seen wrens do the same before: for once his tail was not up, but well down, and he gave his hinder parts a real sousing. Then he paddled all round and across the bathing pool, drenching the whole of his small body and splashing the water over his back with his short, blunt wings. After this he stood on the edge of the bath and preened his feathers for a few moments: then he went in again for another thorough wetting. So dabbled\were his flight feathers that he flew only with difficulty to a stone, where he shook himself free of moisture and then impetuously departed. The whole pantomime was acted with amazing verve and energy. We felt that he enjoyed his bath as much as we enjoyed watching the perform-ance.

Starlings have a mass mentality, as their feeding habits and amazing congregations at roosts reveal. So it is not surprising that they indulge in mixed and communal bathing. I have seen seven in the

Opposite : (*above*) Hedgehog
(*below*) Female adder with young

bath together, jostling and splashing each other; needless to say the bath was nearly emptied.

There are sometimes bird bathing tragedies, but not by drowning. One morning while we sat at breakfast a kestrel was hovering above our lawn; as this had frequently happened I did not pay much attention; but all at once I was aware of a commotion in the bird-bath, which is on the edge of the flags just outside the window, and there was the kestrel with its wings outspread over the bath and a blue tit in its talons. The hawk flew off carrying its squealing victim. It was a case of Murder in the Bath. Usually the kestrel is a mouser: often on the cliffs I have watched wheatears and pipits fulfilling their lawful occasions heedless of a kestrel hovering overhead.

One summer, when a pair of nightingales had their nest near our garden, one of them frequently used our bird-bath, generally towards evening. She tubbed very thoroughly, spreading her russet tail feathers and wings and dipping her head with a sideways motion. At such close quarters her large, dark eyes, betokening her crepuscular habits, were noticeable. She usually preened after her first dip and then returned for a second. Probably she came off her nest at this time for recreation and refreshment.

Many species of birds came to drink at the bird bath and quite as often in cold as in warm weather. A mistle thrush drinks delicately, sipping small, dainty beakfuls; as he lifts up his head you can see his spotted throat ripple while the water trickles down; a lovely sight, and incongruous in a bird which looks so ungainly as he hops about the lawn.

We have never had much luck with our nesting boxes; they seem to attract only blue tits, though we had hoped that a pair of nut-hatches, which at one time became very tame, might use one of them. I watched a brood of blue tits fly from the nesting box in the cherry tree at the end of the lawn. They appeared in turn at the entrance hole like little jacks-in-the-box. Most of them on their first flight reached only the macrocarpa hedge, some half a dozen yards away, but one hardy adventurer got as far as another cherry tree ten yards off, and then flew strongly some thirty yards further to the roof of our house. When the nestlings have flown, both they and the parents disappear absolutely from our garden, and we usually see no more of them till early autumn. I believe they take their broods to the woods where they feed on caterpillars: I have watched family parties thus engaged in the late summer.

An open nesting box on the south side of our house is sometimes patronised by spotted flycatchers. One year the newly hatched family

Opposite : Wood-warbler at nest

came to a sad end: in the evening the five youngsters were being tended by their parents and all seemed well. But next morning I noticed that the old birds were not going to the nesting box and examination proved that the nestlings were dead and cold. They were in good condition, and I could only surmise that a sudden change of weather, bringing cold wind and rain, had chilled them. I have heard of other similar misfortunes. Spotted flycatchers do not arrive here till the weather is comparatively warm, which suggests that low temperatures are unsuitable for their offspring.

Another year the eggs were destroyed in the nest while we were away from home. Suspicion fell on jays, whose ruthless methods recall the evil deeds of a Hitler or a Cesare Borgia. However, after an interval of not more than a week, the flycatchers took heart, and a second clutch was laid: the eggs hatched out and the young got off successfully.

These flycatchers have endearing habits: the nesting box was just below one of the windows of our bedroom, and in the early morning we often heard a slightly guttural but mellifluous conversation between the pair which was no doubt of a connubial significance. The cock fed the female and not only after the act of mating but when she came off the nest during incubation. Drinking at the birdbath they sipped fastidiously at the pool's margin.

The young after leaving the nest were fed by the parents in the vicinity for several days. I once saw an old bird give a cabbage white butterfly, which was swallowed, wings and all, to a fledgling: it is no wonder that the young birds cast up pellets of such indigestible material.

A precocious youngster from one brood left the nest prematurely and performed a rather untidy parachute descent upon our lawn. I placed him on an outlying bird table beyond the reach of predatory groundlings; there he clung precariously in a high wind for most of the day. Once he fluttered down to the lawn, tucked his head into his shoulders and went to sleep.

A garden kept under daily observation sometimes harbours unexpected visitors. Looking out of my study window one morning when a deluge of rain had made a watercourse of a garden path, I was delighted to see a grey wagtail, in winter plumage, tripping along the edge of the water; a new visitor to our garden, for we are some distance from a stream. As I was watching it a small school of some half-a-dozen long-tailed tits trickled desultorily along the macrocarpa hedge near the lawn and down an avenue of crab-trees. And then suddenly a male black redstart, in very dark plumage, descended on the grass and began feeding. He was almost at once attacked by an impertinent sparrow and driven off, but returned and perched for a moment on the bird-table. I was lucky to entertain three such welcome and unaccustomed visitors in the course of a few minutes.

Goldcrests occasionally visit us: they pry about in the macrocarpa hedges. One morning a neighbour brought over to us a hen gold-crest which had struck her window and then fallen down upon the sill outside. Its eyes were nearly closed and I feared that it would not live for long. Warmth was the only hope, so my wife made a nest of shavings and lint in a small hamper and put it by the fire. The bird revived at once, opened its eyes and stood erect. I left it in the room where my wife was writing; she told me that after about ten minutes it found its way out of the hamper and flew up to the top of a corner cupboard; thence it fluttered from one point to another—the picture rail, stag's antlers, and tops of picture frames. Its favourite perch was the back of a toy donkey, nearly one hundred and twenty years old, which stands on the cupboard. But though all the windows were open it failed to find its way out. Finally, after more than an hour, a bird flew across the window outside and a dunnock piped up. This seemed to attract the goldcrest's attention, for it darted through the open window and was gone. Probably this bird was suffering from shock. Its recovery shows how warmth and care will sometimes save a bird's life.

There are no more delightful visitors to our garden than gold-finches. In winter they join the blue tits in feeding upon birch trees. As they pull to pieces the female catkins the discarded seeds, whose sheaths roughly resemble in shape a fleur-de-lis, float to the ground on a pair of fairy wings; delicate food for dainty birds. I have also seen goldfinches taking the seeds from our dwarf lavender hedge; their taste must be aromatic. Groundsel they love—and thistles: we grow both, inadvertently.

CHAPTER II

'SMALL DEER' ON EXMOOR

But mice and rats and such small deer
Have been Tom's food for seven long year
KING LEAR

Exmoor is famous for its red deer, but it has its 'small deer' also. Some of them inhabit or visit our garden near Porlock. Short and long tailed field-mice are a perennial and inexhaustible nuisance. They devour my sprouting peas and broad beans in contempt of all the deterrents so fulsomely and fatuously advertised in catalogues and gardening papers. Rabbits, in spite of wire netting, invade us: the does make their 'stops' preferably in the rose garden, or failing that in the strawberry bed, or near the roots of a peach tree. Leverets I have found more than once in the long grass, but they quickly disappear when discovered: I believe the mother hare removes them: but they learn so soon to run and then 'clap' that it is possible they themselves instinctively leave the form when disturbed. Rats we have, I hope, eliminated for the present, but it needed continual watchfulness to prevent them infesting the old hedges bounding our land when first we came into occupation. They seem to be omnivorous; a Porlock man once told me that two fair-sized trout were swept down the mill leat to a grating that was partly stopped up with débris, so that a pool was formed above it. He saw two rats come to the pool, and one of them seized a trout in the middle of its back and carried it off.

They, and mice and voles also, are no doubt kept down by stoats and weasels; both are frequent visitors to our garden. At breakfast one morning we saw a stoat come running along the garden path; he followed a line to a clump of saxifrage, and nosed into it. At first he seemed to find nothing, so he made a cast round the base of the macrocarpa hedge; then he dived into the clump and began scratching: we could see his hind legs straining as he dug. Soon he emerged with a young vole in his mouth, which he proceeded methodically to devour, beginning at the head. When he had nearly finished this morsel he was disturbed by the arrival of the postman and dived to cover beneath the macrocarpa. When all was quiet again he reappeared, finished the first vole and extracted a second; this he also consumed, and then a third, and a fourth. He quested about for more, but finding the cupboard now bare, he retreated whence he came. I examined his excavations and found that they ended at an opening between two stones which was too small for him. The birds on the lawn, twenty yards away, took no notice of him whatever. Eating, he crouched head down, like a cat; he licked his chops after the meal and scratched himself with a hind claw. The whole performance revealed a cold-blooded efficiency.

In winter I have occasionally seen stoats with white or partly white pelts on Exmoor, but never so far have I observed this change in weasels. They still retain their customary brown. In winter in the Clyde district I have seen weasels with almost pure white coats. On Exmoor white is seldom for long a protective colouring.

There is some ground for believing that polecats exist on Exmoor. A few years ago rabbits were found on Ley Hill which had been killed by bites larger than those made by a stoat; a keeper about the same time reported similar injuries, and I have had accounts from two eye-witnesses of an animal, larger than a stoat or ferret, pursuing rabbits. But so far as I am aware there has as yet been no definite identification of a polecat in this district.

Weasels also help to keep down vermin. While I was shaving one morning, a weasel ran out from underneath the macrocarpa hedge, stopped and looked round warily, with upraised head. Seeing no enemy, it slithered sinuously up the path and arrived at the corner of the wall which bounded what was then the rose garden. Here it made another cautious survey of the country, and then, dashing across to a clump of pinks on the edge of a bed, disappeared into a hole. In some thirty seconds it reappeared, carrying in its mouth a plump, and very lately deceased field-mouse. 'Pop went the weasel' down the path and out of sight. I measured the mouth of the mouse-hole afterwards and found its diameter did not exceed four-fifths of an inch.

The Body Odour of the weasel must be noisome in the extreme, for another day when a neighbour's terrier hunted one round our garden, and ran it to earth in a dry dyke wall, there was a tearing scent and a fine cry from the one hound. We dug the quarry out and the terrier well and truly killed him: perhaps it was a pity, having regard to the way in which the other weasel dealt with the field-mouse. But unfortunately weasels are also fond of fattened fledglings; there were the beginnings of a nest in the hole whence we ejected this one, so probably his killing was warranted: a brood of young weasels would have cleared our garden of nestlings.

This terrier was a dog of character: though low of carriage, his gastronomic tastes were above his station. He once made a Lucullus banquet of one pound of raw cod and the better half of a plum cake which he found negligently deposited on our back doorstep. As his mistress insisted on repairing his depredations by the gift of a more expensive and larger cake, we should have welcomed a repetition of his offence. This did not occur again, though he swallowed a squash racquet ball which had to be removed by a surgical operation. His name was 'Brandy'.

The West Somerset name for stoat or weasel is 'varey', a word which seems to have affinities with 'viverra', the Latin for ferret. (Incidentally, Cinderella's glass slipper was really fur, *pantoufle en vair* being mistaken by the translator from the French for *en verre*.)

I have only twice found an adder in our Eden. One August day a boy killed a young one which he found basking in the sun on the concrete outside our garage. Another, a female by its size, I found sun-bathing in our south hedge. Both may have come from Pool's Wood, only a few hundred yards away.

I once slew a grass snake, three feet long, in a neighbour's garden. Its effluvium, emitted *se defendendo*, was overpowering: it must have rivalled the weasel's B.O.

Of slow-worms there are plenty. Sweeping up some dead leaves on the drive in October I disturbed what at first sight seemed to be a thread of live quicksilver. It wriggled and squirmed itself over the gravel with such whiffling activity that it was with some difficulty that I succeeded in capturing it between finger and thumb. This live wire, silvery above and black below, was a young slow-worm, two to three inches long. Early in September we had seen an adult 'blind-worm' sunning itself on a clump of saxifrage which borders the drive: probably this youngster was one of its progeny. After inspection I released it where I had found its parent; for the slow-worm, though often destroyed as a snake by the ignorant, is, of course, really a lizard without legs and quite harmless. And it is a good friend to gardeners for it loves a diet of slugs, particularly the small grey slug *limax agrestis*.

Under a board laid on the ground in the garden as a trap for slugs is a nest of red ants (*myrmica rubra*) and with them are always in summer several young slow-worms in various stages of growth. There is a similar nest and the accompanying slow-worms under a slab of slate. The slow-worms seem to live amicably with the ants in their nest. When the board or slate is removed they worm their way beneath the surface and disappear.

The association, if it exists, between ants and slow-worms, seems curious. A friend who is an authority upon ants tells me that it has not been discovered whether there is any reciprocity in the association, but he does not think there is. No known enemy of the slow-worm would be kept away by ants, nor is he aware of any way in which the slow-worm could be beneficial to the insects. The ants crawl over the slow-worms and this does not seem to be resented. The eye is the only portion of a slow-worm's anatomy that would be vulnerable to ants' attack.

A slow-worm which I once dug up from a heap of rotted grass shammed dead at first, but when I put it down, uncurled and crawled away.

One evening recently I saw from my windows a magpie killing and eating something on a grass path beyond my lawn. When I went to investigate, the bird flew off carrying what looked like part of a snake. On the spot where I had seen the magpie I found no snake, but a portion of a slow-worm, still wriggling. Though magpies will attack and eat almost anything, including worms, slow-worms do not seem to have been recorded among their diet. What was left of the 'blind-worm' was subsequently attacked by a cock blackbird and presumably consumed, as I could find no trace of it later.

I have never met with a lizard in our garden, but in a lane not far away my wife and I surprised a brown lizard sunning itself on the flat surface of a tree stump. With tail curved in a semi-circle, and its tiny claws extended, it lay absolutely still while we watched it at a couple of yards distance for several minutes. But for the throbbing of its throat and flanks as it breathed and the blinking of its jewelled eyes, it might have been cunningly carved in wood or bronze.

Toads are always welcome in gardens, for they counteract the disregard of malthusian principles among slugs. Usually when disturbed they withdraw with a gait which suggests injured dignity. But it was a surprise when removing the top of a nest of the all too common field vole one morning to discover a stolid toad in possession. Many years ago I found one in the nest of a yellow-hammer about a foot from the ground: he was sitting upon two of this bird's eggs, one of which was squashed beneath his belly, but the other intact. I have read of toads in a robin's, a hedge sparrow's and in a song-thrush's nest, the last situated some distance up a holly tree. I once saw a toad fall quite six feet from an oak. It began to climb again almost at once, and progressed three feet up the trunk in a quarter of an hour, resting after every few minutes' advance. Evidently the climbing powers of toads are considerable. No doubt other people's nurseries make snug quarters: to eject an imperturbable toad must be a difficult proposition for either a bird or a mouse.

Toads are easily tameable. One which inhabited a hole in the rough stone edging of a path in my garden became tame enough to take slugs from my fingers. Another which lived in a lettuce frame accepted worms from me; he would snatch at them, but sometimes he missed and got a mouthful of earth instead, which he removed with his front toes and by licking his lips with his pink tongue.

Toads appear to be fond of music. A correspondent in *The Times* once described how he lured nine into the house by playing his guitar. Some years ago, when on summer evenings a trio of violin, piano and 'cello was playing, I have known six toads assemble on the lawn and in the bird bath just outside our open windows; their rapt expression betokened enjoyment, but we did not invite them indoors.

Hedgehogs we welcome: they are gluttons for slugs. A mild day may wake them from their winter hibernation and stir them into activity. One December, after a period of east wind, I found a hedgehog snugly curled up in a 'nest' of dried grass at the bottom of a hedgebank in our land. It shivered slightly when I touched it. Subsequently the weather turned milder, and I found the nest empty. Search showed that the hedgepig had built another dormitory at the bottom of a thorn hedge some forty yards away from the first one. It had crawled into an oblong tunnel of herbage—a rough and ready sleeping bag—and had stopped the entrance with a bunch of dried grass. My interference with its original winter quarters had been resented, so during the mild spell it had changed them. In July of 1940 a hedgepig came to the flags outside the garden door, after dark, and consumed saucers of milk provided for him. We watched him lapping slowly, with an accompaniment of snufflings and gurglings which betokened appreciation. He always licked the saucer clean.

Red squirrels were uncommon in the district when we came to live at Porlock. They seem to be one of those species which are subject to periodical fluctuations. But during the last few years we have gratefully observed an increase in Eastern Exmoor. Today there are at least ten squirrel haunts near Porlock.

When a red squirrel goes hoppetting along a woodland glade he seems a live particle of russet fern. Scampering up an old oak, his claws his climbing irons, he hangs parallel with its trunk, with which his tawny coat and brush harmonise so completely that he might be a loose strip of raw bark. Soon he leaps to a crotch near the bole and suns himself, the light shining through the fine hair tufts which top his cocked-up ears. Enjoying the warmth, he doses—as squirrels often do—with half closed eyes and nodding head. A cloud shrouds the sun; he wakes suddenly, and nibbles at a nut in his front paws, and then scurries off from branch to branch along a squirrel track which to the human eye seems giddy and precarious, but is to him as safe as tram-lines.

In cold weather squirrels retreat to their dreys—balls of twigs, leaves and bark shavings—which doubtless form a very snug retreat. They do not hibernate in our district: severe weather may render them comatose, but a mild spell revives them and they resume their normal life. Even in snow I have seen their tracks, in which the needle-sharp nails are so marked, crossing plank-bridges in Horner, and elsewhere.

Indeed, to lapse into semi-somnolence seems to be a squirrel habit, and that not only in winter. One afternoon in May, my wife and I watched a squirrel in Horner Coombe. He came hop-skip-and-jumping along the edge of the stream, stopping now and then to drink, and shaking shining drops from his whiskers afterwards. Then he climbed an ivied trunk, from whose recesses he extracted hidden nuts, and nibbled. After this somewhat scrappy meal he curled himself in a furry ball on a fallen trunk and dropped off to sleep. Possibly these attacks of drowsiness are, during winter, a symptom of the hibernating instinct, but at other seasons they are simply the natural relaxations in a life which is lived very intensely. A squirrel is almost bird-like in his constant expenditure of nervous energy and joie de vivre.

His tantrums are amusing: he flies off into impotent fits of rage at very small provocation. My wife and I once disturbed a squirrel in the act of making a cache for a walnut. He slithered up the smooth bole of an ilex tree as a fish slips through water, and from his perch swore and chattered at us like an angry kitten; in his rage he beat upon the trunk with his fore and hind feet and swished his besom tail from side to side; his whole frame quivered, his throat throbbed with passion. 'The little pot boils over in that way', as Hudson said.

To watch a squirrel climb a tree trunk at close quarters is thrilling; the muscles ripple rhythmically up his back and bulge like knots on his forearms. In spite of his apparently hair-breadth escapes in the course of his aerial acrobatics, he rarely makes a mistake. I have only once seen a squirrel fall, and then the odds were against him. I was with a friend, and the squirrel had taken refuge in an oak standing solitary in a meadow. After his manner, he put the tree trunk between us and him, so my friend walked round to the other side of the tree while I remained where I was. In the attempt to hide from both of us he missed his footing and fell with quite a heavy thud on the ground, but, to our relief, ran off at once, apparently unharmed.

Is it a fancy that in the squirrel's character and make-up we can trace some of the attributes of Pan, the roguish god of the woods, released from servitude to earth? At any rate it was such a fancy that suggested

PAN IN THE TREE-TOPS

Wearied of clumsy goat-hooves, Pan arose;
He skipped to Circe's Isle, besought her change
His uncouth body. Dropped his curving horns,
Coarse goat-hairs moulted; acrid scent dissolved.
Instead grew pelt of russet; for his horns
A pair of little cunning cocked-up ears;
Eyes, lewd and leering, melted, dark and mild.
She gave him claws for hoofs; a brushwood tail
Curled shadow-fashion over rounded back.
He shook himself and blinked. A glassy pool
Mirrored a pygmy Pan, a lissom sprite.
No more he shambled, sprang on sinewy legs,
Saw a smooth pine-hole, red and raw from showers;
Leapt, scampered up it, claws dug deep in bark,
With muscles rippling down his sinewy back,
Like winds a-ruffle over tawny fern:
Snatched at a cone, sat hunched upon a branch,
Blew (minding Pan-pipes held to goatish lips),
Nibbled and scattered scales. Then suddenly
Started and frisked, and leapt from twig to twig,
(What fun for Pan, earth-free, to cling and climb!)
Swung pendulous at dizzy heights, and chased
—A mad arboreal kitten—after leaves
That naughty winds had driven scurry-mad.

. . . . . .

Pan's pipes are silent now, amid the trees;
But when he whisks his besom tail, and scolds,
Rogue-eyes a-twinkle, squirrel still is Pan.

On Exmoor we are, I believe, so far free from that pest, the grey squirrel, a tree-rat, which is responsible for the disappearance of the red in some districts. A visitor to Exmoor told me that in the autumn of 1937 he saw a grey squirrel near Bossington, but personal search and enquiry have failed to discover its presence.

As we were returning from Horner Green one evening some boys told us that two mice had come out of a nest in the hedge: they were, of course, dormice. They had emerged from a ball of leaves and bents built about four feet up; their furry coats were a beautiful tawny brown and their tails were long and hairy. They climbed about the small branches or twigs, clinging by their small strong claws and by curling their tails round the branchlets. The parents we did not see: probably they were in hiding. However soundly the dormouse may sleep at times (and one hibernated snugly in a Porlock kitchen all one winter), these youngsters were very wide awake: their beautiful dark eyes were brilliant as they watched us.

Badgers are elusive beasts: there are plenty on Exmoor, but it is difficult to get a sight of one. I still remember spending a couple of hours up a tree outside a well-known earth, or 'bury' to use the Somerset name, and being rewarded only by the sight of a grey shadow disappearing in dusk that was almost darkness. I have never seen one in our garden, but they inhabit a wood near, and a special policeman met one ambling along our lane one winter night.

I have only once attended a badger dig; it is a sport which does not attract me, but it seemed too good a chance to miss of meeting brock at close quarters, and on this occasion the badger was to be bagged.

Terriers were put into a large 'bury' beneath an old hedge: almost at once something emerged in a hurry, but it was fox, not badger. The same thing happened at the next earth. A move was then made to a larger bury which had several entrances. There brock was at home: listening with ear to the ground, we could hear the terrier barking; the badger was trying to dig himself in with the terrier in hot pursuit; brock as he dug made a scuffling sound; the terrier's frenzied excavations were heard as a series of thuds.

At intervals holes were dug down into the bury behind the subterranean combatants, the object being to insert a spade at brock's rear and thus force him to bolt forward into an open sack when the terrier bayed him; eventually these tactics were successful and the badger was bagged.

Usually a badger's tunnel is made between the shillets, i.e. loose stones on the surface, and the soil below, but sometimes his bury is beneath the 'mores', a West Somerset name for roots, of a large tree. I know one Exmoor coombe where badgers must have lived for hundreds of years: its sides are honeycombed with their excavations and there are mounds of earth two or three feet high outside the entrances.

A countryman with whom I got into conversation a year or two ago told me that badger's fat melted down was green in colour, and was an unfailing remedy for cold in a cow's udder. I have never tried it.

In *Wild Exmoor Through the Year* I stated that the boar badger has only five front teeth in the lower jaw and that the female has six. I now find that this is an error, arising from a misunderstanding of the descriptions of a badger's dentition in a plate in Mr. H. Mortimer Batten's book *The Badger Afield and Underground*. Correspondence with Mr. Mortimer Batten revealed the fact that the boar's skull with only five front teeth in the lower jaw, shown in the plate, was not typical: the animal had lost a tooth. Mr. Mortimer Batten tells me, *in lit*, that to the best of his knowledge six is the normal number in both sexes. He adds that they are rarely complete except in a young badger.

Cats we do not encourage: they and birds do not agree. The lethal habits of a cat belonging to a Porlock lady caused her considerable pain. After the animal had killed two tame robins it was deported to Cutcombe, some six miles away across the moor, as the crow flies. It returned to its home, very tired, a fortnight after; if it followed the most direct route it must have crossed Dunkery. But with a reserve of nine lives to draw upon this is not remarkable.

CHAPTER III

MERLINS ON EXMOOR

I was once in a cinema when the next picture announced was 'Merlins at their nest'. Someone sitting behind me asked his companion 'What is a merlin?' 'I think it's a snake,' was the reply; I could not resist turning round and saying, 'No, it's a bird'.

In *Wild Exmoor Through the Year* I wrote of Exmoor merlins, but since that book was published I have had further opportunities of observing their habits and learned much about them which I did not know before.

Some of these merlins have used the old nests of crows, ravens and other species for breeding; but others have chosen to nest upon the ground. Very often, if the situation chosen is a crow's nest, it is one built in a not very high tree, low down in a deep coombe. This position doubtless conceals the breeding place from the prying eyes of human enemies; but the observer is often able to watch the nest from the coombe-side. One such nest was an old grass-grown carrion crow's only some eight feet from the ground in an ancient, weather-beaten thorn. On a June morning I and two friends could look down on the hen merlin brooding her eggs for three hours at a distance of some twenty yards.

As we watched she held us with her large, dark eye, but never stirred an inch. Field-glasses revealed her every feather, her mottled buff and brown mantle and barred tail, her yellow cere and bluish beak. She did not always sit head to wind, perhaps because in that position she would not have been able to keep her eyes upon us, but she was extraordinarily tame.

A few days later when I visited the place with two other companions, we found the jack merlin brooding. He was much shyer than the hen, nor did he show her maternal solicitude for he flew off from the nest as soon as we appeared, and did not return during the quarter of an hour we remained. Shaded by the foliage, when brooding, the sheen of his plumage was dulled, but in flight his slate-blue wings gleamed azure in the bright sunlight.

Three young merlins were hatched out in this nest. The coombe lay in a very lonely part of the moor, and I enjoyed the peace of solitude while I watched their fascinating ways. But one day, some three weeks later, solitude was rudely marred by a sudden irruption of hikers—I counted fifty as they crossed a ridge—evidently out on a communal walk. These mass excursions may have their attractions for those who, like rooks, jackdaws and other talkative people, prefer to take their exercise in flocks, but to the field naturalist, who prefers to dawdle and look at whatever happens to interest him, they are usually a dreadful experience. A day out with a Field Club, for instance, usually means that most of your time is taken up in keeping the too inquisitive away from bird-rarities whose whereabouts you are anxious to conceal from collectors, and prevent the banderlog from disturbing birds with their chatter.

The young merlins, now about fourteen days old, were queer, owlish-looking little creatures. The tail and wing feathers were well grown, but there were puffs and tufts of greyish down still adhering to the head and back which gave them an unkempt, rather rakish appearance. They sat round the nest in a circle, with tails inward: now and again they crawled about, glaring at me balefully with their large blue-black eyes; then, concluding that my presence was harmless, they cuddled up to one another and dozed.

A fortnight or so later they were fledged and had left the nest. When I arrived one was perched on a tree in the coombe near the nesting site. Soon the jack merlin appeared, flying with prey in his talons; his call was answered by a shrill, peevish 'kee-ing' from the young ones. The jack tried to pass the prey to one of them in the air; on the first attempt the tyro failed to grasp it, but on the second essay the youngster bound to the morsel. I cannot find that this passing of the prey by the old to the young has been recorded by any other observer, but there was no doubt about it. In fact I saw the same thing happen an hour later. Another time the cock brought the prey to two young who were on the old nest and dropped it there; a fine squabble for the meal resulted.

Two years later what was probably the same pair of merlins nested in another thorn tree in the same coombe, not fifty yards distant from the previous site. As the last young bird flew from this nest before July 7th, the first egg of the batch of four was probably laid about May 8th; this is a rather early date, for incubation sometimes does not begin till the 3rd week in May. Not far from the nest I found the partly feathered leg of a bird whose identity puzzled both me and the naturalist who accompanied me; finally we recognised it as belonging to a young cuckoo, and there can be little doubt that it had fallen a victim to the merlins. In 1937 I found the remains of a young cuckoo on the hunting ground of another merlin couple: these gawky, overfed fledglings must fall an easy prey to these swift and keen little hawks. I have seen feathers of a blackbird at plucking places and the wings of the Emperor moth, but most victims of merlins are small birds.

Tracking down nesting merlins is a fascinating pastime, for the discovery of the nesting place, especially if this is situated upon the ground, is difficult. You may constantly see the birds haunting a patch of moor and yet be baulked in running to earth the sitting hen, for, as will have appeared from what I have already written, she sits very close.

For three years we saw young merlins on one part of the moor, after they were fully fledged and strong on the wing, but never could find this nesting place. So in the spring of 1936 my wife and I decided to concentrate on this quarry.

In mid-May I put up the jack merlin from a stone in a clearing where the heather, burned a few years before, was still short. There were many castings—pellets of feather and infinitesimal bones—round the stone, and further on was the corpse of a slaughtered meadow pipit. The jack circled high, his vivid blue plumage glinting in the sunlight, until I lost him against the sky's blinding brightness.

A week later I walked the area methodically: a hen-harrier glided past me as I approached the clearing, but though I again found castings, I saw no merlins. Early in June I once more caught a glimpse of the jack coasting with spasmodic wing-beats along the edge of woodlands that fringe the moor, but still he gave me no clue. A few days after I had, for the first time, a distant view of the hen, but she performed the vanishing trick as completely as her mate.

Owing to enforced absence it was early July before my wife and I could make our next visit. This time the scent was stronger for we roused the hen merlin from her kill of a cock chaffinch, and she keened 'kee-kee' in shrill anxiety. Evidently there were young somewhere about, but again we searched for them in vain.

Two days afterwards she flew up near the same spot and circled round, bitterly complaining. We watched for an hour and more and in the distance saw the jack pass prey to her in the air: his cry as he met her was more plaintive than her harsh screaming; but once more she eluded us. Tantalised by these happenings we came the next day: three times did we see the hen, but again we returned baffled.

My next free day I determined to solve the mystery if I stayed out till dark. Again the hen got up where we had so often seen her. Her cries were redoubled, and she seemed more anxious than before. Soon after the jack appeared, but both birds vanished in a dip of the moor below me.

A shower came on, and I sheltered under a gorse bush while I ate my lunch. This over, I stood up, and at once heard the hen 'kee-keeing' below me and to the left. Walking towards her, I espied a tiny piece of white down tangled in a sprig of heather. Advancing into the wind, I found another fragment of fluff, then another. Scent was growing hot. After some fifty yards, this feathery trail led me to a scattered patch of white down in a heathery dimple. From it two fledged young merlins rose, and flew unsteadily up the hillside. And in the heather was yet another youngster—crouching over the head and wings—of a plucked goldfinch!

He was a lovely bird. Though unable to fly, his featherage seemed complete. The dappled brown and grey plumage of his back and wings was powdered with a bluish sheen. His orange legs and feet were tipped with jet-black claws. And then his large dark eye, wild and fierce and defiant! Handled, he turned on his back and menaced me with claw and beak, but calmed down as I stroked his head.

Spilt down led me, alas, to another dismembered goldfinch, and eventually to the original nesting place, upon the ground, beneath tall heather, by a wind-tortured fir sapling; there was an addled egg trodden into the ground.

Calculating backwards over the incubation and fledging periods, it appears that when I first put the jack up in mid-May the hen must have just begun to sit. We must, in our searches, have often passed within a few yards of her.

These young merlins, having survived so far, had a good chance of reaching maturity; would their prospects have been better had they been reared in a tree-nest? The tree-nesting habit, in so far as it protects the eggs and young from ground-haunting enemies, works for the survival of the species: but a tree nest, especially when it holds young in white down, is easily discovered by man. Merlins are courageous in defending eggs or young from intruders; I have seen them drive off herons, ravens, buzzards and crows, and I have no doubt they would tackle a stoat, a hedgehog, or an adder. But badgers are said to eat eggs and nestlings: they and also foxes, are common in the tree-nesting merlins' country, and I fear that even those brave little hawks would be unable to repel a raid by so formidable a marauder as reynard or brock.

In 1938 I found a merlin's nest on the ground in tall heather. It contained four eyases recently hatched. Six days later the nest was empty; there were no signs of bloodshed or destruction. It is possible that the disappearance of the young was due to human agency, but either badger or fox may have been the culprit. Security from

the latter type of enemy may explain the origin of this arboreal nesting in certain localities. Again, in 1937, a merlin's ground nest was destroyed, probably by a deer or a pony stamping on the eggs, for I found the broken egg shells in the scrape. This is another danger which arboreal sites escape.

The tree nesting habit would in time produce a strain of birds that preferred such a situation and eventually the custom would become universal with their descendants.

Though in winter merlins leave the moorland which is at that time almost deserted by the meadow pipits and other small *passeres* which are their principal prey, they evidently visit their old nesting haunts. In November and December 1936 I found droppings and merlin's feathers near the fir sapling by the nesting place of the previous summer, and the same was the case in the following March and April.

In the spring merlins begin to frequent the area that is chosen for the nesting site later on. Towards the end of February 1938 I went to the coombe in which ravens had nested two years before, hoping to find signs of their intention to nest there. Though I saw the ravens, the old nest had not been repaired; but while I was walking up the coombe a hen merlin twice glided past me. Twice in March I saw both jack and hen in the same place. For various reasons I was unable to go to the coombe during April, but on May 4th the hen merlin appeared on the skyline as soon as I reached the coombe. She was evidently uneasy at my presence, for she pitched on the thorn and rowan trees growing there and watched me intently. I waited to see whether she would give me any hint as to the nesting site, but as she merely kept me in view I climbed the rowan tree which contained the old ravens' nest and found in it two merlin's eggs. I had suspected that this site would be chosen, though I believe these merlins were the pair which had nested on the ground less than a mile away in the two previous years. As one of these nests was that in which the eggs were trampled by deer or ponies the birds may have decided to try a safer situation.

Some ten days later I found the hen incubating four eggs, two of which were of a lighter colour than the original pair. She did not leave the nest until I had climbed nearly up to her; her behaviour was curious; she fluttered clumsily through the branches, and seemed—I prefer not to be more positive—to adopt something very near the 'broken-wing' tropism, flying low above the heather and spreading out her tail. By this time the rowan was in full leaf and the ravens' nest was quite invisible until I was directly beneath the

Opposite: Another view of Old Porlock

tree, another example of the protection afforded by the arboreal nesting habit.

I visited the site on several occasions during incubation but never stayed long, as I did not wish to disturb the birds. On one occasion five buzzards appeared above the coombe; both the jack and the hen at once attacked them furiously, stooping at them from above and harrying them until they departed to a safe distance. The merlins' speed enabled them to out-pace and out-soar the buzzards, who, adopting their usual method of defence, turned on their backs and presented their talons to the enemy. One buzzard, in avoiding his tormentor, turned a complete side-somersault. The brave little jack even tackled two buzzards at once.

On June 9th the nest contained four young recently hatched, in the first yellowish-white down; their eyes were just open and there was an empty egg-shell in the nest. By the 21st they had acquired the grey down and the brown primary feathers were sprouting. Three were defiant: they sat up and hissed at my camera with open beaks. The fourth eyas crouched limply at the bottom of the nest. I have noticed before that a merlin brood often contains one weakling. On the 28th the youngsters were almost fully fledged but there were still tufts of grey down adhering to the brown feathers; one was still less vigorous than the rest of the family. After another week's absence I found the nest empty and the eyasses were not visible; they were probably in hiding but by this time the foliage was very thick.

I found very few kills near this nest; those which I saw were greenfinch and whinchat. Usually there are many plucking places near the nesting site. Old anthills are used for the purpose, but in this coombe there were none, and the kills I found were on dead thorns and on rocks.

In 1936 friends gave me information about a merlin's nest in another coombe, and on 1st July I found the hen sitting on four eggs in an old raven's nest in a thorn. This is a late date, but the eggs were a second clutch laid after the first clutch had been robbed by some kleptomaniac from a tree nest about a mile away. While watching this nest I saw the jack merlin when driving off a buzzard actually drop his claws upon the buzzard's back. I once flushed the jack from these eggs, but when the young were hatched he did most of the hunting. He usually passed the prey to the hen in the air—once when both birds were almost over my head—but sometimes he deposited his victim on an ant-heap and the female gathered it from there. Almost every anthill on the side of the coombe opposite to the nest had been used as a plucking place: one was a veritable shambles; the kills included skylark, wheatear, whinchat and meadow pipit. Red-backed shrikes were feeding fledged young in bushes near the nesting tree.

Most authorities say that the merlin usually makes no real nest, and I made the same statement in *Wild Exmoor Through the Year*. But I have since discovered that this is not entirely correct. The wool lining of the ravens' old nest in which the merlins nested in 1938 had quite disappeared, and there was a distinct subsidiary nest inside the ravens' structure in which the merlin's eggs were laid. The other 1938 merlins' nest, on the ground, was not a mere scratching nor a fortuitous collection of twigs; it was a definite nest composed of fine heather bents. The photograph facing p. 65 shows the young when partly fledged in the old ravens' nest. In an earlier photograph, unfortunately not clear enough for reproduction, some portions of the subsidiary nest were just visible. By the time the later photograph was taken the subsidiary nest had been trodden into the structure of the ravens' nest.

I have on at least two previous occasions found merlins breeding in an old nest of carrion crow or raven from which the wool lining had not disappeared. In both cases the merlin's eggs were laid upon the original lining and no new subsidiary nest was constructed. Evidently it was not considered necessary.

My notes on the courtship of merlins are scanty. In early May I once watched a pair flying around a patch of heather near an old nesting site. The jack uttered a note resembling 'tchok', which I had not heard before, and the hen, besides giving the usual 'kee-kee-kee' call, sometimes keened a curlew-like whistle. In courtship the jack chases the female: when eventually she settles, perhaps on the top of a thorn tree, he swoops upon her and mates her there.

All the merlin nests which I have described above were in moorland country where grouse were breeding, but at the plucking places I never found any grouse feathers, nor have I ever seen any evidence of merlins destroying these or any other game birds. Yet in spite of this I know that merlins and their nests in this district and elsewhere are destroyed by keepers. There is a certain type of keeper who will slay any hawk at sight, regardless of whether it takes game or not. Mr. J. W. Seigne in *A Birdwatcher's Notebook* writes that he once saw a merlin carrying a young bird which his keeper insisted was a grouse. The keeper fired, and the merlin dropped—not a grouse but a young merlin, which it had been trying to carry into safety! It is significant that the percentage of merlins recovered under the British

Birds Marking Scheme between 1909 and 1941 is 19·9 per cent. The percentage of recoveries in the case of even so black-listed a bird as the sparrow hawk during the same period is only 14·0 per cent. I commend these figures to the sympathetic consideration of those game preservers—and there are many—who love and take an interest in birds other than those which are preserved for sport. Keepers are often ignorant men who know no better. A word from their employers would stop this senseless persecution and give a fair chance of survival to one of the most beautiful of our British falcons.

CHAPTER IV

SPRING MIGRATION OF SWALLOWS
IN SOUTH WEST ENGLAND

Dr. Eagle Clarke, in his *Studies in Bird Migration* writes that migrant birds after they reach our shores follow a multiplicity of routes in seeking and returning from their inland seasonal haunts. He adds that the majority of these are mere by-paths which can be known in any district only to naturalists who have long resided in it and have paid close attention to the comings and goings of the migrating species which visit their countryside.

The members of the Bird Watching and Preservation Societies of Devon and Cornwall respectively have, with the valuable co-operation of the *Western Morning News*, for some years past paid special attention to the spring migration in their districts of certain specified species. One of these is the swallow; as a result of these investigations it has been possible to discover and map out many of these by-paths in Cornwall, Devon and west Somerset. As I have been responsible for co-ordinating the records of the arrival of this species, a summary of the results from 1934 to 1942 is of some importance and perhaps of more than local interest. A comparison of the movements observed during this series of years gives a good idea of the general trend of the spring swallow migration in South-West England.

The major factors in migration are the meteorological conditions where the flight begins; if birds arrive when circumstances here are adverse it is probable that the flight started when conditions were favourable but deteriorated *en route*. The information available as to continental weather conditions when compared with the arrival of swallows in the South West showed that though these birds generally take advantage of favourable weather, they sometimes cross the Channel when meteorological factors are adverse. High winds are unsuitable, but a light or moderate wind, even if contrary, does not seem to hinder their passage if other circumstances are propitious. Swallows are strong fliers. It must also be remembered that much migration takes place at a great height, and at these higher altitudes bird travellers may reach favouring air currents.

A flying man once told me that at 4800 feet he met a skylark ascending: he added that aeronauts, when they see birds, often ascend into the following air currents in which the birds are flying.

Coward wrote that a bird can be and is carried on a moving current of air, and any exertion that it makes speeds it up, and helps it to travel faster than the current that bears it. He believed that when migrants are seen coming from the sea flying against the wind we see them *because* the wind is contrary; during the crossing they have met with adverse winds and have dropped to a lower altitude to avoid trouble. We do not know the nature of the wind and weather at the starting point.

First, as to the duration of swallow migration: this shows a rather surprising uniformity, for in each of the nine years it has lasted practically two months. The respective dates are: 1934, March 29th to May 27th; 1935, March 29th to May 28th; 1936, March 22nd to May 31st; 1937, March 19th to May 19th; 1938, March 19th to May 21st; 1939, March 18th to May 30th; 1940, March 11th to May 15th; 1941, March 27th to May 27th; 1942, March 14th to May 31st. A single 'freak' swallow seen on March 4th, 1935, near Torquay, may be disregarded and another on June 10th, 1939, flying north north west near Exmouth, is exceptional. Generally, swallow migration in the west extends from the 3rd or 4th week in March till the 3rd or 4th week in May. Each year the early arrivals of swallows are few; it is only later on that there are especially active periods, during which the birds come in waves or rushes.

Some ornithologists hold that birds follow definite fly-lines or routes: others believe that they travel on a broad front over all the country lying between their breeding and winter quarters. I do not see why both theories should not be correct. But the nine-year records show that in the western peninsula many swallows take well-defined routes.

The main routes are shown on the map on p. 40 which is adapted from maps which appeared in the *Western Morning News* and in *Discovery*. They present some interesting problems. The 'West Coast Route', which probably begins at the Isles of Scilly, passes along the north-west and north coasts of Cornwall, Devon and west Somerset. In most years there are accounts of swallows arriving as far south as the Isles of Scilly; in every year they have passed along the greater part of this route to the north-east or east. But there are deviations; in 1934 eleven swallows departed from Tresco, Isles of Scilly, in a south-easterly direction, a course which would take them to Ushant on the Breton coast. Did they there join the continental migration route which skirts the western coast of France, and proceed northward? Again, in 1936 some swallows departed north-west from the Isles of Scilly, a direction which would lead them to Ireland.

Also, in 1934, a swallow flew north-west from St. Agnes, on the north-west Cornish coast: the nearest land in that quarter is Ireland. In 1935 and 1936 on the west coast of Cornwall, north of Land's End, swallows were seen flying in a southerly or south-easterly direction: these birds may, on reaching the shores of southern Cornwall, travel northwards along that coastline.

In several years there were records of swallows turning south or south-east from various places on the north-west Cornish and north Devon coast, and from the directions taken it is probable that some of these travelled up the valleys of Taw and Torridge. In May 1938 and in April 1939 at Widemouth, south of Bude, some swallows turned inland to north-east, away from the migration route northwards along the coast. Evidently some swallows follow the West Coast Route so far and then leave it, presumably for their breeding places.

Some swallows turn away from the north Devon and west Somerset coasts in a north or north-westerly direction, a course which would bring them either to Ireland or the south coast of Wales. Thence they may join the well-known migration routes along the western shores of Wales or the east and west coasts of Ireland.

Others leave the West Coast Route at various points on the north Devon coast and fly westward to Lundy, where they have been seen arriving. In 1935 and in 1938 most swallows reached Lundy Island from the south-west and left to the east or north-east; those flying east might join up with the easterly route along the south side of the Bristol Channel; the others would reach South Wales.

Mr. Richard Perry, who stayed on Lundy Island during the spring and summer of 1939, states in his book *Lundy, Isle of Puffins*, that in that year the migration of swallows on Lundy was from S. and S.S.E., i.e. from the direction of Hartland and the north-west coast of Devon and Cornwall, and that they invariably passed on to N.N.W., or N.N.E. There were rushes on various dates in April and May which usually coincided with the waves noted on the mainland.

The migration on Lundy in 1939 reached its maximum intensity at noon on 20th May, when Mr. Perry estimated that swallows were travelling north at the rate of 5000 an hour. The total number of swallows traversing Lundy during the spring migration he thinks may have reached sixty thousand. Rushes took place mainly on fine, calm days. Migration began to diminish at the end of May, though occasional birds departed northwards till June 29th. A few were seen flying south in July and north even in September; these late movements are difficult to explain; perhaps they were flights by non-breeding birds or birds of the year, or possibly were caused by bad weather.

In 1938 and 1939 attempts were made to trace to south and west Wales the routes taken by the swallows flying northwards from the north and north-west coasts of Devon and Somerset and from Lundy, but the results were inconclusive. Some arrivals of swallows at various places on the south and west coasts of Wales coincided with their passage north-west up the Exe Estuary, northwards along the river valleys from south Devon, and along the west coasts of Devon and in west Somerset. Since the war few Welsh records have been available.

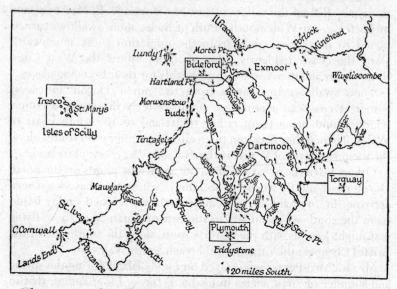

The reports for all the nine years again reveal that there is a passage of swallows both east and west all along the southern shores of the Bristol Channel from Porlock to Morte Point, west of Ilfracombe. Many of those flying east along this route are continuing their journey by the West Coast Route, but others, and also many of those proceeding westward, must have come overland, some by river routes from the south Devon coast, mentioned later, and others directly across Dartmoor, Exmoor and east Devon. There are in some years definite records of swallows flying north and north-west and from east to west at Black Torrington in the Torridge valley towards the north-west and west Devon coast, and from the Yealm and the Erme valleys in south Devon round the west side of Dartmoor; some have been seen passing over Dartmoor and Exmoor at altitudes of 1000 to 1500 feet and others going north-west up the Teign Valley and near Wiveliscombe.

A possible explanation of the origin of the West Coast Route suggests itself to me. Any physical map of the British Isles and north-west France shows that the fifty fathom line runs in a broad curve to the east and then to the west from the Isles of Scilly to Ushant on the west coast of Brittany. Within comparatively recent geological time this must have formed the coastline of south Britain and west France. We do not know when bird migration began, but it is probable that in those days migrants followed that coastline. Do they still uncon-sciously do so? It is significant that such a route would guide them to the Isles of Scilly and thence to the present West Coast Route.

Turning to the south and south-east coasts of Cornwall and Devon, there is evidence of swallows migrating northwards up the St. Erth valley from Mount's Bay to St. Ives, up the Fal valley, and overland near Grampound in Cornwall. The five rivers—Lynher, Tamar, Tavy, Plym and Meavy—which eventually debouch into Plymouth Sound—are all popular swallow highways: two swallows at sea on April 2nd, 1937, twenty miles south of the Eddystone, flying north, would reach land at Plymouth. Small parties that flew in from the sea at Stoke Point, east of Plymouth Sound, in May 1938 and 1939, and another arriving east of Prawle Point in April 1939, passed north, a direction which would take them up the Tamar, Yealm and Erme Valleys, and across Dartmoor. In fact, those are the general directions of flight here, and of swallows following the Dart River or reaching the coast near Torquay. Others came in from the sea in 1939 and 1940 at Paignton and at Start Point.

Those passing up the Exe estuary and valley (a very crowded highway) and up the Otter and Sid also fly north. Two were seen separately at sea off Budleigh Salterton in April 1935, flying north-west. Others flew in from the sea at the same place and near Exmouth, Torquay and Dawlish in 1939 and 1940.

A glance at the map of Western Europe shows that the coast between Plymouth and Torquay juts out into the English Channel and would therefore naturally form the first landing place of many northward bound birds which had followed the well-known fly-line along the west coast of France.

In the spring of 1939 I was able through the kindness of M. Jacques Delamain, to get in touch with ornithological correspondents in western and south-western France. Their records, extending over seventeen years in some cases, show that swallows arrive in Charente Inferieure (La Rochelle, Rochefort, Marennes) about March 15th, and continue their passage till the end of April or mid May. There are occasional arrivals at the end of February. In Vendée (Aiguillon-sur-

Mer, St. Jean de Monts, Bourgeneuf, Fontenay le Comte) advance swallows appear as early as 9th-12th March, but the main body comes ten days or more later. The route taken is along the west coast of France, but there is a parallel flight inland.

In northern Brittany the dates of first arrivals vary from March 25th to April 17th, the average being the end of March or first week in April. There is a flight line from Pte de Primel to the N.E., i.e. towards the Channel Islands and Cape de la Hague (Manche).

M. Baal (Conservateur du Museum de Jersey) informs me that there are three flight lines from Brittany across the English Channel: (1) The strongest, entering England on the S.E. Coast. (2) From Cape de la Hague N.E. to the Isle of Wight. (3) A weaker and later flight, from Cape Frehel in N. Brittany, N.W. to Start Point in Devon. The third would be the route taken by swallows arriving over the sea on the south Devon coast, as above mentioned. After their arrival in Devon the river valleys must provide plentiful shelter and sustenance for some of those whose bourne is not yet reached.

It is interesting to find from these records that in some years swallows were seen in south-west England at dates earlier than those of their arrival in south-west France. In 1940 the first swallow was seen at Porlock on March 11th, one day before the first arrival at La Rochelle. The next appeared at La Rochelle on March 17th, but none after that date until the 24th. In the meantime I received eight swallow records from Cornwall, Devon and Somerset. These, and other reports, suggest that some of our earliest swallows in the south-west peninsula may fly to us direct from Spain, instead of taking the flight-line along the west coast of France.

But there are a good many reports of other swallows flying roughly east or west along the south Cornwall, Devon, and Dorset coasts, near Mount's Bay, Plymouth, at Stoke Point, Start Point, across the Exe estuary and on the Fleet near Weymouth. These birds seem on arrival to coast along our shores, but it is impossible to conjecture their ultimate goal. Some may eventually turn northwards either up the river valleys or overland.

Several instances have occurred which show that migrant swallows are sometimes driven back by bad weather after they have arrived. In *British Birds* for July 1938 Major Dorrien-Smith wrote that on June 2nd he noticed an abnormal number of swallows at Tresco, Isles of Scilly; on June 3rd the numbers had increased to thousands. At noon that day he steamed out into the Atlantic to the north, and met several batches of swallows travelling south as on autumn migration. At 5.0 p.m. there were several thousands of swallows at Tresco.

Weather was unsettled: on 1st June there had been heavy rain with wind N.E. and then S.E.: in the evening there was a 70 m.p.h. gale from N.W. Numbers were much reduced by the 5th and on the 8th June were normal. Weather became warmer on the 6th.

On 29th May, 1938, in the afternoon, there was a steady drift of swifts and housemartins and a few swallows down the Exe Valley from Dunster to Tiverton, i.e. due south, and at 5.0 p.m. twenty-five swallows flew high southwards. The morning was fine but there was rain in the afternoon.

On 9th April, 1937, twenty-four swallows were seen flying southwards in small parties down the coast at Bedruthan near Newquay against a stiff south wind and driving rain. Some other instances of migrant swallows flying in a direction contrary to their presumed destination may, perhaps, be explained by their having arrived at night and overshot the mark, and so having to return by day to their goal. But much swallow migration takes place by day.

Mr. W. B. Richmond, in *England's Birds* says that the instinct to migrate is innate in every bird, and the individual is a pawn in a universal movement of colossal magnitude; but once the movement has started the problems occurring on the journey must be solved by the bird as an individual: it is in the behaviour of the individual rather than of the mass that we are likely to find the real secret of migration. And he goes on to state that we shall only solve the riddle of migration when we come to understand the bird, and conversely the fact that migration is still a riddle shows that we have as yet made scant progress towards elucidating the minds of the birds we pretend to watch. I am sure we shall never solve it by regarding the bird as a mechanical automaton acting under the impulse of a blind tropism.

Theories about bird migration are numberless: but all are theories, and no more. What do we know of the urge which sends myriads of beating wings forth upon their long journeyings? All is conjecture: but as we watch birds on spring migration it is surely their eager, poignant happiness which strikes us. It is their home-coming; they seek the same patch of countryside—spinney, river, hedgerow or common—which is their home.

> *God gives all men all earth to love,*
> *But since man's heart is small,*
> *Ordains for each one spot shall prove*
> *Beloved over all.*

Kipling's lines are true of birds as well as men.

CHAPTER V

TALES OF AN EXMOOR VILLAGE

Pictures of Porlock some seventy years ago show us a primitive
country village. There were two-storeyed cottages, white
washed and thatched, with spacious, built-out fireplaces, and
tall chimneys sprawling up one outer wall; barns and farm buildings,
ranged haphazard alongside of narrow, devious streets paved with
cobbles. Between and in front of the houses were flower gardens.
By the bridge stood the mill, and opposite to it was a square building
called the market house. On market days sheep and cattle were
penned with hurdles in the village street and inside the market house
were erected 'standings', stalls for the sale of sweetmeats and other
dainties. Round the churchyard wandered a row of somewhat
decrepit cottages; they covered what is now part of Parson's Street:
the entrance to the churchyard passed beneath the first floor of one
of these dwellings. The mill stream provided the sole water supply
both for drinking and washing purposes. I have been told that one of
the village inns brewed its beer with water taken from this stream
not far below where it received the effluent from certain stables.
That an epidemic of diphtheria occurred is hardly surprising.

Much of old Porlock has been swept away by modern improve-
ments. Some still remains: there is the lovely old Doverhay Manor
House, now the Doverhay Reading Rooms; the gabled Royal Oak
Inn dates from 1704; the exterior of some of the old cottages
remains unaltered. Others have been pulled down, some after
destruction by fire, within the last ten or fifteen years. No doubt
many of these old buildings were inconvenient and insanitary, but
it seems regrettable that new buildings could not always have copied
the simple dignity of the old. It is not difficult with a little fore-
thought to combine beauty and modernity in architecture though the
fact is too often ignored in this kaleidoscopic era. Some buildings
have been reconstructed with understanding of and sympathy for
the *genius loci*. Of others the less said the better.

The Church with its curiously truncated spire, remains unaltered
as to its exterior since mediaeval times, except for the chequered
walls of the vestry. There is a tradition that the top of the spire was
blown away in a gale about the year 1700. Dr. F. C. Eeles believes
that this must have been the famous gale of 1703. Irreverent

romancers embellish this bald statement of fact by asserting that the portion so removed settled down on the roof of Culbone Church, which accounts for the pepper-box belfry on that quaint little edifice. Others explain that when the damaged steeple was being repaired the stag-hounds ran through the village in full cry; naturally the Porlock men engaged on the tower downed tools and followed the chase; when this was over they decided not to proceed further but, in local parlance, to 'let un' bide'.

The oak shingles, with which the steeple is covered, were after fifty years renovated in 1933, for after a high wind they had begun to fall 'like leaves in Vallombrosa'. Some of the main internal timbers, surely hewn from Porlock trees, have lasted for seven hundred years since the tower was built in the 13th century.

A village situated almost at the extreme westerly end of west Somerset, and on the borders of wild Exmoor, was inevitably isolated in the days when communications were difficult. The railway has never approached nearer than Minehead. The roads were not, until comparatively recent times, very efficient. An old man, now dead, who had worked on the roads all his life, told me that he could remember when the Lynton Road up Porlock Hill was no more than a country lane, and that he himself had helped in most of its widening. It is only the motor-car which has within the last twenty years made such villages easy of access. Naturally in such circumstances there was much intermarriage. The result is that many of the older families are intricately related; after twenty years we are still discovering unsuspected affinities. Some women of the older generations have never or rarely visited villages only a few miles away and know little of the moor except in the immediate neighbourhood. Residents of twenty or thirty years' standing are still 'foreigners'. In the course of a recent conversation two Porlock men were discussing a new arrival. 'What nationality is he?' 'Oh, he's a Wiltshireman,' was the reply. A further result of long isolation is the different character of the population of villages separated by no more than two miles, and the animosity they sometimes show towards each other. But these are delicate subjects.

In the old days smuggling was rife along this unfrequented coastline. It was, in fact, a highly organised industry which everyone winked at, even if they did not participate in it. In his *History of Part of West Somerset* the late Sir Charles Chadwyck-Healey, gives an account of the way in which trade in smuggled goods was carried on at Minehead and Watchet and describes how hiding places for smuggled goods existed at Bromham, a lonely farm up Hawkcombe,

Upper Doverhay Farm, a cottage at West Porlock and in a field near Pool's Wood.

A Porlock man recently told me this story. A keg of smuggled brandy was taken to a cottage at Chapel Knap, Porlock Weir. Word was brought to the tenant, an old woman, that the customs officers were coming to search the house. When they arrived she welcomed them, seated on the brandy keg which was covered by her ample skirts.

'Come in, my dears, you be welcome to search wherever you do please, but there baint nothing here.' Nor did they find anything.

There was also smuggling at Ashley Combe, where there was a path from the house down to Rock Cottage on the beach. Warning would be given when the Customs men were in the village and the goods would be stored safely away. On another occasion two vessels collided in the Bristol Channel and both sank. One was carrying rum, and the casks were washed up on the beach. Men from Porlock tapped the liquor from the casks into kegs which they hid in Culbone Woods. Unluckily they somehow forgot to mark the place where they were concealed and could not find them when the Custom House officers were safely off the scene.

Those were wild days: I have been told by one of Porlock's 'oldest inhabitants' that within his memory some of the men who dwelt in the remotest parts of Exmoor, 'out over' as they say, had their hair and beards cut only at sheep-shearing time. If any Exmoor inhabitant considers this statement libellous, I am not responsible for it. But such straws show where and how the wind blew.

Another story, gleaned from the same source, reveals that even as late as the end of the 18th century there were some lawless characters at large in this countryside. My informant was not far off eighty, and the tale was told to him as having happened in her youth, by his grandmother, who lived to be over ninety; this carries us back to some 150 years ago.

There is an ancient Manor House called Bratton Court a few miles from Minehead. In those days pedlars used to go round with their packs, and one of them called at the Court and asked permission to leave his pack there till he returned for it. A shoemaker's apprentice was living in the house, and there was a rule, which was rigidly enforced, that apprentices were not allowed a candle to light them to bed. However, this boy had secreted an illicit candle-end, and when everyone was asleep he came downstairs in order to repair one of his boots, and sat down on the pedlar's pack; to his amazement he felt something move in it. He roused the master of the house and the rest of the household; they found that in the pack a man was concealed. They tied him up, loaded the blunderbuss and awaited events. Soon they heard the confederate's whistle outside; they fired the blunderbuss in that direction and in the morning found blood on the ground. The cunning plot to admit burglars to the house had miscarried.

In Bagley Combe, near Langcombe Head, there is a ruined cottage, whose derelict garden still contains flowers, and some decayed outbuildings. The tale I was first told about this house was that it was deserted because the inhabitants at some remote era all died of plague. But the story current in Porlock is of a more recent happening and seems to be the true explanation. The last inhabitant was a man who lived there all alone. One day three men from Porlock, in a drunken frolic, went to the house and told the solitary man that he had been caught sheep stealing, a crime which in those days meant at least transportation, and that he would shortly be arrested. He was entirely innocent of this offence, but the dread of arrest and punishment so preyed upon his mind that he hanged himself. After that no one would live in the cottage as it was supposed that the suicide's ghost haunted the place.

The burning of the ashen faggot on Xmas Eve is still observed on Exmoor and at least by one family in Porlock. A friend has given me a description of the ceremony in which he has often participated. It is a family affair and the whole household assembles in the kitchen. The faggot is of green ash, five or six feet long and two or three feet in depth. It is tied round with withy bonds and placed on the open hearth upon the top of the cinders. It burns until morning and the heat is so great that you have to hold a newspaper before your face. As each bond breaks there is a drink of cider all round; hence bibulous families tie many bonds. (Teetotallers prefer cocoa.) Every person in the room sings a song or tells a story, or recites.

The ceremony has obvious affinities with the Yule Log: the custom was on Xmas Eve to light a heavy block of wood, called the Yule Log, with a fragment of its predecessor that had been kept throughout the year for that purpose. Authorities differ as to whether this rite had a solar origin or was purificatory: if the former, it was a piece of imitative magic. Like the Midsummer fires, it was intended 'to ensure a needful supply of sunshine by kindling fires on earth which mimic the source of heat in the sky'. Naturally Midsummer and Midwinter, the times when the sun's heat begins to wane and wax, would be the appropriate times for these kindlings.

In 'Somerset' (Cambridge County Geographies) it is stated that the Ashen Fagot Ball, a festival long kept up at Taunton, was believed to commemorate that chilly night when the soldiers of King Alfred found, to their joy, that green ash branches made excellent camp fires. But the similarity of the rite to the Yule Log ceremony suggests a more ancient origin. It is perhaps significant that Ygdrasil, the tree of life in Scandinavian mythology, is an ash.

In *Wild Exmoor Through the Year* I mention the quaint Somerset superstition that rupture in a child can be cured by passing its body through a split ash sapling. Culpeper, in his *Complete Herbal*, recommends a decoction from ash leaves for 'slimming' and as a cure for snake-bite and other dulcet diseases: he also refers to the belief that 'there is such an antipathy between an adder and an ash tree that if an adder be encompassed round with ash-tree leaves, she would sooner run through fire than through the leaves', but adds, 'the contrary to which is the truth, as both my eyes are witness'.

An old Porlock resident told me that 'the old people' used to say that if you waved an ash stick in a circle round an adder, and said a charm, the adder could not pass outside the circle. Evidently this is another form of the same superstition. All this testifies to the ancient belief in the ash's magical qualities.

Other old superstitions still linger even today. A young Somerset woman recently told me that she once made butter on Good Friday and it went bad. She said it was supposed to be an unlucky day and that, though she did not 'hold with' superstitions, she should never again make butter on that day.

Two folklore fragments are enshrined in these local rhymes:

> *Don't wash your clothes on Innocents' Day*
> *Or you'll wash all your friends away*,

and

> *If you buy a broom in May*
> *You sweep all your friends away*.

The younger generation on Exmoor, when you mention witchcraft, say 'Oh, the old people believed in it but of course we do not'. But it is still imbedded in their sub-conscious minds: some of them are more than half-believers in it.

A West Somerset farmer's wife, extant within living memory, suffered from acute indigestion: she firmly believed that a toad or lizard, or some such reptile, resided in her stomach and devoured everything that she ate. This tale leads on to another. Many years ago a Cambridgeshire friend told me that a bargee, with whom he was conversing in a village inn, declared that he had never taken physic, but if he felt ill he swallowed a small live frog. My friend bet him he would not do it then, so the man went out, found a small green frog and swallowed it alive and whole. The bargee went on to tell of a local man who lived in a damp house where frogs were always hopping about; one of them jumped up on the settle beside him; he took it up and swallowed it, but immediately went out and vomited violently. My friend suggested that this did not speak well for the frog cure. 'Ah,' said the bargee, 'it weren't a frog; 'twere one o' they toads.'

West Country folk are a long-lived race: we have many married couples who, if they would not perhaps qualify for the Dunmow flitch, have lived amicably together over a long series of years. That this is not always the case may be inferred from two tales told to me by a West Country parson, father of an old school friend, many years ago. A brother cleric called on an old couple in his parish who had recently celebrated their golden wedding, to proffer his congratulations. He found Darby alone; Joan was out shopping. 'Yes,' said the ancient meditatively, 'us 'av bin married for fifty year, fifty year.' He paused and then added viciously, 'An' I wish I'd never seed (seen) 'er!' The same cleric visited another parishioner to condole with him on the recent loss of his wife: in the course of conversation he suggested, as some palliation, that 'the Lord had need of her'. The response was unexpected. 'Well,' said the bereaved, ''E be welcome to 'er: she were a teasy toad.'

A final story, told to me by a West Somerset friend, shows that the blessings of civilisation are still unappreciated by some of us. The local blacksmith in a certain village (not Porlock!) was asked to speak over the telephone to the M.F.H. He did not know how to use the instrument. When he was shown the receiver he said: 'I can't speak into thicky danged thing: I just been ettin' onions and 'e'll smell my breath.'

Local names are always of interest, There is a decrepit orchard, much haunted by small birds, on the slopes of the stream at Bossington: it is called 'Buckland'. A meadow on the south side of the same stream, below Mr. John Acland's house, is picturesquely known as 'Dinderduck'. On Pentley Hill, near the stone seat, the place where a spring runs over the path is called 'Didley Dab': it is the same stream which runs down Halse Coombe and some people say that Didley Dab is where that water crosses Hacketty Way above Burrow Hayes Farm. The allotment field in Hawkcombe, Porlock, was known as Hallelujah field because at one time the men who sang in the church choir were given allotments there.

After heavy rain a pool of water often forms in a hollow in the middle of a field near Hurlstone Point. This field is called 'Mare Meadow': the lowest point of it is below the level of high tides; only the broad, high shingle bank keeps the sea out. Two other fields a little further west, similarly low-lying, are called 'Marlands'. These names suggest a derivation from 'mare' or 'mere': the shingle has, of late years, silted up towards this eastern end of Porlock Bay, but at one time no doubt all these fields were frequently flooded both by sea and land water.

In a district where the rainfall is usually some forty inches, rain is naturally much in our minds. We even make rhymes about it. This one was, some thirty years ago, said and sung by Porlock children:

> *When the mist comes from the sea*
> *There won't be rain to drown a flea;*
> *When the mist is on the hills*
> *There's rain enough to drown the mills.*

The latter couplet is true enough to my own knowledge, but I have known deluges on Exmoor come from the north-west off the Bristol Channel, and in fact from almost any quarter.

All the eastern portion of Exmoor is now under the ownership or control of the National Trust and will always be unencumbered by buildings. Its aspect today cannot have greatly changed since the time when it was a Royal Forest. This, however, does not apply to the southern slopes of Selworthy Beacon. There is (or was) in the Holnicote House Hotel a landscape showing an older Holnicote House, and the country behind it, viewed from somewhere near the highest point of Ebb's Hill Lane; the date of the picture is about 1750. The artist has exaggerated the height of Selworthy Beacon and Bossington Hill, but the lower slopes of both are shown entirely bare of trees. The story is that one of the early Aclands prudently planted a fresh piece of woodland whenever another baby was born.

It is the shingle bank along Porlock Bay which keeps out the sea from Porlock Marsh: probably at one time it came much nearer to the village and the Marsh extended further inland. Today there is a ceaseless conflict between sea and shingle. The voice of each breaking wave is soft: it slithers up the high piled bank, caressing every rounded pebble, but in recession it snarls and hisses, enraged by thwarted endeavour. Gradually the senses are lulled by this rhythmical ebb and flow. It can be heard a mile or more inshore when the wind is from the sea—a lovely sound to listen to on a still evening when smoke hangs in a tenuous pale-blue film above the roofs of the village, and from the moor a curlew flies, crying.

CHAPTER VI

'CONSIDER THE CHAFFINCH'

Much has been written by ornithologists about the rarer British birds, but the commoner species have, by comparison, been rather neglected. Mr. W. B. Richmond in *England's Birds* remarks how rarely we pause to consider the charm of our common birds, and how little we know about their private and individual lives. It is a good plan sometimes to 'consider'—in Lord Grey's sense—some bird which we see every day. We shall find that familiarity has made us overlook many interesting characteristics: we may even make one or two unexpected discoveries, for not even the wisest pundit knows everything about birds. So let us 'consider' the chaffinch.

Writing for bird lovers it is unnecessary to state that the plumage of the cock and hen chaffinch are entirely different. But I was astonished, when trying some years ago to interest village boys in the local bird-life, to find that they were ignorant of the distinctions between the sexes. And, indeed, the tyro might be excused if at a first sight he found it difficult to believe that two birds, one so smart and the other so dowdy, were male and female of the same species.

The cock chaffinch is a lovely bird, deserving of Mrs. Browning's line 'no chaffinch but implies the cherubim'. And yet how seldom the beauty of his plumage is brought out in the plates which interleave ornithological works. Thorburn's picture is the best which I know, but even his fails quite to suggest the delightful way in which the manifold hues shade almost imperceptibly into each other; nor does any artist seem able to inspire his colours with the lustrous radiance which glows through each feather when the spring is in the chaffinch's blood. Probably only an impressionist artist could succeed. 'Slate-blue', the usual description of the head and nape, quite fails to convey the brilliance of their tints; 'chestnut', a bright chestnut, is a more appropriate epithet for the cheeks and back. The rump is a luminous green such as is only found in the bark of some smooth trees, and certain mosses. The virility of this colouring becomes apparent when we find that in chaffinches which are in other respects total albinos it still persists as faint yellow.

The breast and underparts vary, according to season, from rose to pink, in nuances of infinite delicacy: this colouring attains its purest quality in the young cock when changing into adult plumage, for then the breast has the blush of the wild rose. And on the wings, in addition to the gay shoulder knot, there are freaks of primrose and faint edgings of brown upon black only discernible when the bird is tame enough to come to the hand or within an arm's length. The pure white of the outer tail feathers forms a foil to the grey and black of the inner ones, which are cunningly margined with green. Surely, if the chaffinch were a rarity, men would journey from afar for a sight of it and it would be rightly appraised as a jewel among birds.

In contrast to all this splendour the hen seems a dull and insignificant creature. Indeed, apart from the white bars on her wings, she wears no gaudy plumes, But her sober fawns and browns have their own quiet beauty: she shares with her mate the greenish shades on the rump and sometimes her breast is faintly flecked with rose.

Here, on the borders of Exmoor, and also in my garden, the chaffinch is our commonest bird, more plentiful even than the abhorred house sparrow, or the greenfinch. I found the same conditions in a district of North Wales some miles inland from Abergele many years ago. It occurs in the higher parts of Exmoor up to 1350 feet, but is not so plentiful there as at lower altitudes. I have a note that in May in the course of a walk from Simonsbath to Cow Castle in the Barle Valley, some years ago, I saw only one chaffinch. In the parts of Norfolk which I have visited I have not found it present in such large numbers as in west Somerset; the same applies to some districts of Sussex, Cornwall, Bucks and Huntingdon. On Lundy and Skokholm I found it scarce or absent, though Mr. Lockley records a large migration on the latter island due east in October 1936.

Linnaeus named the chaffinch *fringilla coelebs*—the bachelor finch —because he believed that the hens deserted the cocks and migrated southwards, and Gilbert White frequently mentions the immense preponderance of hens in winter flocks in the Selborne neighbourhood. It is rather curious in the face of this that, after searching my notes for the last 34 years, I find that only on two occasions have I seen flocks in which females preponderated; these occurred in the Exmoor district. Both here and in Cheshire, where I lived for twenty years, winter and autumn flocks were made up either of mixed sexes, or males were in the majority. It may be that the tendency to form what an old cynic called the 'Monstrous regiment of Women' prevails only in certain localities. Collett, in *The Heart of a Bird*, says that the chaffinch congregations of one sex only are migratory and that they pair up at the nesting place. But, as will appear later in this book, my own experiments with ringed chaffinches prove that some remain paired throughout the year.

In winter chaffinches consort with gatherings of other species. In Cheshire they mixed with bramblings in the beechwoods, and near Porlock I have seen both species feeding on the flotsam on the margin of the Marsh after flood-time. One of the largest assemblies of small *passeres* which I have ever encountered were busy among the débris of manure and straw scattered on a pasture at West Porlock. It was a gargantuan miscellany of chaffinches, greenfinches, bramblings and linnets, divided into two unequal portions. The larger I estimated at a thousand (of which quite fifty were bramblings) the smaller at four or five hundred. The birds swarmed as thick as ants at an ant heap; they were almost touching each other. The hedges of the lane next to the field were evidently used by the flock as roosting places: they were covered with whitewash. In the lane I found six kills of chaffinches, probably the victims of a merlin which had been seen lately in the neighbourhood. Evidently he had found good hunting.

The furious voracity with which these birds were feeding was a little uncanny: there was a ruthlessness about it, as of a murderous mob which has got out of hand. Competition was intensive and there were occasional fights. I saw one greenfinch hold another upon the ground for some seconds and peck it furiously. It was January, when daylight is short, not more than eight hours, and during that space birds have to stoke up for the ensuing sixteen. So while they feed it is every bird for itself and the weakest go under.

Stackyards are a very present help in trouble to chaffinches in a hard winter. There you find them associated with all the small fry of tits as well as with gaudy yellow hammers and greenfinches, not to mention the ubiquitous house—and rarer and cleaner—tree-sparrow. Occasionally they keep company with goldfinches; when they rise together in sunlight their wing-bars flash in a glitter of gold and silver.

I have heard the song of the cock chaffinch in every month of the year. In Cheshire the earliest date was the first week in February, but often in severe winters there was no full song until the middle or end of that month and sometimes not until March. Here at Porlock I nearly always hear chaffinches singing in January: my earliest record is January 7th, but more usually they are silent until the second or third week. Moorland chaffinches, living at higher altitudes, begin and end their song period later. These early songs are invariably short, consisting of only the first phrase; sometimes they are husky, and so soft that they are hardly audible, like the 'recording' of cage birds; but the songsters practise assiduously. They tie more and more knots in the melody. One cock that I heard practising on the first day of February began with only four notes in the first phrase, but gradually increased them to five or six. By the end of January or the beginning of February most birds have added a second phrase, though some late starters have still not progressed beyond the first lap. And with practice the second phrase becomes longer.

Lord Grey, in *The Charm of Birds*, quotes Warde Fowler's comparison of the chaffinch's song to a bowler running with quick steps up to the wicket and then delivering the ball. This certainly suggests its rhythm. The complete *ballade* consists of two phrases separated by a short pause. The first is a chromatic phrase, ascending in less than semitones, the second a descending cadence; the length of both differs greatly with individual birds. Usually it is delivered from a perch, but I have heard it when the singer is on the wing and also when on the ground. It is an amazingly robust and cheerful carol. Watch a cock delivering his solo and you will see his small frame quivering with valiant emotion; usually there is a pause of some fifteen seconds between each rhapsody, but once I heard a cock repeat his song without any pause; like the wise thrush, he sang his song 'twice over'.

If every flower enjoys the air it breathes *eo magis* every chaffinch enjoys the song he sings. The complaint has been heard that in time its reiteration becomes monotonous and brain-wearing. I have never yet had too much of it and I am sure I never shall so long as I can hear. There is a story of a poet who in exasperation flung his boots at too exuberant nightingales that kept him wakeful in his midnight bed; but I have never yet heard a chaffinch sing at night.

When once the song season has started, weather has little influence on chaffinch music. A high wind will sometimes stop song temporarily, but even in a cutting easterly blast the stave is often only shortened. Neither cold, without high wind, nor rain have any sobering effect: I have heard chaffinches shouting lustily when the bird-bath is frozen, and even when the distant moor is snow-clad they still raise their voices, though a trifle less heartily.

Song is usually the prerogative of the male bird, perhaps because he is more arrogant, though Kipling described the female of her species as more deadly. The hen chaffinch sings sometimes. Lord Grey (in *The Charm of Birds*) wrote that he once heard one sing. He adds that the song was not remarkable, but it was distinctly a succession of song notes, though not the same as that of a male. There were no signs of male plumage on this bird: it apparently had no mate and he suggests that the performance was due to some physical change analogous to that which occasionally causes male plumage in the female of some species.

My friend H. A. Roy Thomson tells me (*in lit*) that he once heard a hen chaffinch singing in between excited nuptial flights. The song was, in this instance, like a cock's but shorter and richer in tone.

In February 1942 my friend, Mr. S. D. Gibbard, also heard a hen chaffinch sing. The song, which was usually complete but sometimes omitted the normal ending, was repeated thirty times almost concontinuously. The notes were full and round but rather slurred and not so clean cut and definite as the usual chaffinch song, and pitched in a good deal lower key. The bird appeared to have entirely normal female plumage.

One morning in April, while I was dressing, a hen chaffinch pitched on the apex of an annexe just outside my window and sang five or six sharp, quick notes in a slightly ascending scale. These resembled the first phrase of the cock chaffinch's normal song but did not quite reach its brilliance. The episode suggested to me that some such string of notes may have been the original theme from which the typical male chaffinch song has, in the course of ages, evolved. The insistent 'spink-spink-spink' of a hungry or excited cock chaffinch forms, at any rate in rhythm, the basis of the first phrase of his song. Most authorities agree that song began with call notes: this female's phrase consisted of simple sounds resembling call notes strung together, in fact much the same song as that described by Lord Grey.

(In Palæozoic days, when the Earth was still in travail with the birth throes of elemental life, there was no bird song, for there were no birds. We do not know what noises, if any, the primitive amphibians made, but they were probably unpleasant. It was perhaps as well that there were no men on the earth then to hear them.)

Chaffinch song has its dialects: it varies in different districts. Witchell, in *The Evolution of Bird Song*, mentions that Normandy chaffinches' songs differed by several notes from those of Scotland. On the west coast of Scotland in May I found the song shorter than in west Somerset. In Huntingdonshire some cocks shortened their strains: others extended the earlier phrase to even eight notes, while the rest of the ditty was of the usual length. In a district of west Sussex some sang longer and others shorter solos than is customary. In Regent's Park I noticed some chaffinches lengthening the first and contracting the second parts of their melodies. Bechstein quotes several variations of chaffinch songs in Thuringia, but these were presumably caged birds, used in singing contests. No doubt individuals have their own vocal idiosyncrasies.

Though I have heard the song in every month of the year, by mid-June the chaffinch chorus is beginning to wane. Sometimes there is a recrudescence of minstrelsy at the end of that month, possibly due to a revival in virility when the cares of nesting and feeding young are over. In July and August the music is fragmentary; the complete song is rarely heard, and it is rendered softly, almost a sub-song. Some of the birds which I have heard and seen in song at the end of the latter month, and also in September and October, are from their plumage birds of the year. These youngsters must obviously have heard the song-themes of their parents and may have learned the notes by imitation: if so, then their first songs are imitative and not instinctive. These strains, and those rarely heard, and only on mild days in November and December, are always shortened versions of the cock's spring carol. No doubt the shortening hours of daylight decrease the stimulus to song.

Verbal renderings of bird-song are rarely satisfactory: our larynx is not a syrinx. In *The Lure of Birdwatching* I mentioned the Artois peasant who rendered the chaffinch's song to a friend of mine as 'J'avais ung tout p'tit, p'tit, p'tit catiaou' (château). Swainsons's *The Folk Lore and Provincial Names of British Birds* gives other French versions. In Orleans it is 'Je suis le fils d'une riche prieur': this is evidently not the full song. In Saintonge the chaffinch asks for 'Un pllein, pllein, pllein p'tit plât de roûtie,' i.e. a piece of bread soaked in wine. About Paris we have 'Oui, Oui, Oui, je suis un bon citoyen'. These suggest longer song-phrases. Perhaps the best paraphrase in English of the complete song is W. Garstang's 'chip chip chip tell tell tell cherry-erry-erry tissi cheweeo'.

As will appear later in this book chaffinches are not early risers. Listening to the dawn chorus in summer, I have often noticed that no chaffinch pipes up until ten minutes or a quarter of an hour after early songsters such as song-thrush, blackbird and robin have wakened with their *aubades*. The eyes of a chaffinch, small compared with those of crepuscular birds, suggest that he's rather a slug-abed.[1]

Bird language is inevitably a matter of inflection. Where there are no words, modulations of tone and pitch are the only way of

[1] Readers interested in chaffinch song will find much detailed observation in the notes by Messrs. M. D. Lister, M. Brooks-King, David Lack and D. S. Falconer in vols. xxxiv and xxxv of *British Birds*.

conveying meaning. Chaffinches have, besides their song, a large variety of 'call-notes' expressing diverse emotions. Some of these sounds I have described in *Here and There with Birds*. The metallic 'spink' or 'pink' (rendered 'chwink' in Mr. Witherby's new edition of his *Handbook*) certainly begins with a sound which is partly sibilant and partly guttural. It betokens excitement, anger, pugnacity, alarm, eagerness. The appearance of food on my bird-table is welcomed both with 'spink' and a shorter, less metallic note, resembling 'wit': it betokens pleasurable anticipation of food. Satisfaction at the end of the repast is expressed by a sound more like 'chip'. My tame chaffinches when asking for pine-kernels utter a note which closely resembles the peevish food-cry of a fledgling, or when doubtful about coming to my hand for food, a sound which is less confident than either 'spink' or 'wit': it betokens indecision.

The greatest variety appears in call-notes associated with court-ship, display and breeding activities. There is the cock's long drawn-out 'weet', repeated at intervals, which is heard only in the mating and nesting season. I always welcome it as a token that spring is, as a matter of fact, here, whatever the temperature may hint to the contrary. The hen, when sitting and on other occasions, utters the same note when flitting back to her nest. Besides this, there is the 'oo-ee' call, the 'ee' being lengthened, also employed by the cock when courting. Pursuing the hen before mating, his emotion is expressed by a guttural crooning, a harsh, reiterated call. She replies in a hoarse chatter: its timbre and pitch vary; it may resemble clucking, churring or chittering. A high-pitched piping is her own summons to a mate for coition. After consummation the cock's song serves as an epithalamium.

The prenuptial display of chaffinches has great beauty, apart from its interest as a piece of avian behaviour. The hen, as she clucks invitation to the cock, strains her head backwards and raises her tail wren-fashion until her small frame is taut as a bow, and at the same time fluffs out all her body feathers and flutters her distended wing-quills. The cock as he advances takes a spiral course, or waltzes round her, with head erect and crest raised and wings and tail depressed to the ground: his very plumage scintillates emotion. It is significant that his courtship attitude closely resembles that adopted when sparring with a rival male. In bird-behaviour one action has often perforce to find expression for more than one emotion. He hovers delicately over her at each encounter. She, unsatisfied, would lure him again to her desire, but his passion, less lasting than her maternal στοργή, fades, and she, *more feminarum*, retires to set her person in order by a thorough preening. Sometimes a cock will fail entirely to respond to the hen's invitation. At other times it is he who does the wooing, but she will not be won.

Once, after consummation, I saw another cock chaffinch attack and drive off the successful suitor. The victor did not approach the hen, nor did I witness anything further to suggest polyandry among chaffinches. But Col. and Mrs. Ryves' discoveries of the deplorable matrimonial tangles in vogue among corn buntings arouse suspicions as to the habits of other species.

CHAPTER VII

THE CHAFFINCH FURTHER CONSIDERED

All birds, and particularly the smaller passerines, are wayward and spasmodic in their behaviour: they have multicoloured minds; ποικίλος, in most of its varied senses, is the epithet which best describes them. And to no bird, except perhaps tits, siskins and goldcrests, is this description more appropriate than to chaffinches. The buoyancy of their flight, the liveliness of their every movement, betoken vivacity. As I watch them on the bird-table, they are 'everything by starts and nothing long': greed, pugnacity, fear, anger, suspicion, succeed each other in kaleidoscopic succession, or even synchronise. In another chapter I have written of my tame hen chaffinch, Gouty; she once flew from her nest to my hand for food, but, half way on her journey remembered her maternal duties and returned, still hungry, to her brooding. I could not quote a better instance of mental instability. Other tame chaffinches when they trespass into my bedroom are constantly torn between hunger (or greed), suspicion, and fear that their retreat is cut off.

I can feel the varied impulses chasing each other in their minds, a mental maelstrom. And all this has its mainspring in a skull which, stripped of feathers, is as fragile as a skeleton leaf.

As a race, chaffinches are pugnacious. Cocks frequently fight their reflections in a window pane. They quarrel venomously among themselves; a male, lame from a bent leg, was at one time the bully of our bird-table: a hen, with an injured and drooping wing was attacked by another female who held her down on the ground and pecked her furiously till I intervened. Another hen constantly chivvied a cock from the table. In contests with other birds they usually come off second best: I have seen them ousted from the table and the bath by robin, cirl bunting, song thrush and even blue tit. Yet at times they show great courage: I have notes of them attacking mistle-thrushes and starlings and once even a kestrel.

Intimate acquaintance with chaffinches compels me to rate them low down as regards intelligence. Their behaviour seems to be almost entirely instinctive. Even those which are now tame took a long time to learn that it was safe to come to my hand for food. The young naturally do not know that glass is impenetrable, but adults never seem to learn the lesson. When they enter any of our rooms they still attempt to fly through shut windows. One of our tamest cocks, instead of walking round a half-open casement to kernels on the sill, spent the best part of an hour trying to peck his way through a pane. A rook or a great tit will learn to haul up a piece of fat attached to a string so that he may feed upon it: a chaffinch never advances beyond trying to perch on the string or snatch beakfuls as he flutters.

Chaffinches, as Mr. Eliot Howard has pointed out, have a strong sense of territory in the mating and nesting season. As early as January or February, according to season, males begin their morning song from chosen stances, one from the elm, another from the roof-tree, a third from a cherry. Later, these challenges are continued throughout the day. Contests between rival males are frequent in air or even on the ground. Nesting sites are selected and guarded. Hens begin to visit last year's nesting site even in February. I have never yet found two chaffinches' nests in close proximity and I do not think I ever shall. Not only the male defends the territory; hens drive off trespassing hens from the nesting area.

Nest building begins the first week in April; my earliest date for a completed nest is the eleventh. It is in my experience constructed by the hen only. I once saw a cock carrying nesting material but cannot say whether the hen accepted it. Her methods are typically described in the next chapter. Egg laying may be delayed for as long as a month in inclement weather. Hen chaffinches are very sensitive to disturbance during the nest-making period. I have known them to desert even after two or three eggs have been laid, but when once incubation has begun they are less fastidious. They sit very closely, only allowing themselves short respites for food. So far I have never seen a cock sharing incubation nor feeding the sitting hen though he is alleged to do both.

'Decorated' chaffinches nests are often recorded. In *Wild Exmoor Through the Year* I mentioned several instances, and hazarded the question whether these did not suggest that chaffinches possessed some glimmering of an aesthetic sense. Since then I have read of another chaffinch's nest adorned with red, white and blue confetti, appropriately at the time of the Silver Jubilee. However this may be, there is no doubt that as an artificer the hen chaffinch is both aesthetically and practically in the front rank among our British birds. Only the long-tailed tits 'pendent bed and procreant cradle' can rival hers. When we consider the embryonic attempts of many other species it is amazing that the chaffinch should have attained to such perfection. The site varies: thorn and macrocarpa hedges in my garden are much favoured: it may be low down in a fuschia bush or twenty feet up in a holly. Messrs. Ingram and Salmon in *Birds in Britain Today* mention one on the ground, and a very curious case of a hen which laid two eggs in a crevice in the bark of a broad horizontal oak branch and tried unsuccessfully to build a nest round the eggs. As will appear in the next chapter a second brood is usual in late May or June.

The eggs vary in ground colour from green to blue. Those in which faint green is clouded with reddish brown are to my eye the most lovely: their hue recalls Meredith's sunset when

the flood
Full brown came from the West, and like pale blood
Expanded.

Text books give four to five as the usual number and occasionally six, seven and eight. I have never seen more than six, and three or four is here the commonest clutch. Incubation may last from twelve to thirteen days and sometimes begins before all the eggs are laid. The fledging period is usually from thirteen to fourteen days but I have known one case of only eleven days, and in another instance, where only one young was reared, the period was probably ten days, but exact dates were not noted.

Chaffinches are very cleanly birds, as is shown by their constant baths even in rain and in the coldest weather. Sanitation of the nest is scrupulously observed, the excrement being removed by both sexes and dropped or deposited at a distance. I have never seen it swallowed. Mortality in newly hatched young is not uncommon, particularly in hot weather. The young are generally fed by both parents, and at frequent intervals, but as will appear in the following chapter, sometimes only the hen fulfils her duty in this respect. When out of the nest, one youngster often attaches himself to one parent only as nurse. The fledglings usually remain about our garden for the first few days after leaving the nest, but after that begin to wander; ringing has shown that in a week or two they may have travelled half a mile. They are fed while in the nest on caterpillars mixed with crumbs from the bird table. Later, it is amusing to see them on the table, wagging their heads and bodies from side to side and worrying their much-enduring parents with importunate cries even after they are well able to feed themselves. Their first attempts at self-feeding are often unsuccessful: they get a crumb in their beak but are unable to swallow it. Soon, however, they learn even to crack hemp-seed, presumably by imitation.

In time the old ones very properly refuse to minister to their laziness. A youngster will often beg from an alien parent, but his requests are ignored or rewarded with a peck which is sometimes resisted: in fact the rising generation soon becomes militant and drives its elders from the table.

Chaffinches are thirsty people. The young, as soon as they are out of the nest feel the need of water: it is curious to realise that nestlings do not know its taste. To watch a fledgling take its first drink is amusing and interesting: obviously it does not know what water is. First it pecks tentatively at the edge of the pool: short sips follow, and in the course of a minute it has learned to drink like an adult.

This ignorance of the nature of water is apparent when young chaffinches first encounter moisture. Sometimes this happens accidentally: like Icarus, the tyro, unskilled in the right management of his *remigium alarum*, crashes into the bird-bath. Surprise soon gives way to pleasure at water's cooling properties: he takes his first bathe, at first half heartedly but then with evident enjoyment. But the first dip is often imitative.

The young cocks soon begin to acquire adult plumage. By the end of July some of their brownish breasts are tinged with pink which by the last week of August is as bright as in the adult. In this they differ from the young hens which show no rosy shades on the breast feathers. In September many young males are in complete adult plumage except for the head which is still brown.

In food the tastes of chaffinches are catholic; crumbs, cheese, and fat are greedily consumed on our bird tables: hemp seeds are held between the mandibles and turned over and over until they crack; the two halves of the shell are discarded. Sultanas they love, and they will dispute with tits over a coconut if they can manage to perch firmly upon it. But the surest lures are pine-kernels (now unfortunately unobtainable) of which they never tire: it is for them that my tame chaffinches fly to my hand and they will catch them in the air if I throw them. With bramblings, they revel in beech-mast; marigold seeds suit their palate. Mealworms I found were an acquired taste. On the moor they devour whortleberries: they hover for flies like a flycatcher. And I regret to have to admit that they play havoc with my green peas.

To analyse the gait of chaffinches is puzzling. They take short steps, which makes their progress look almost like a run, but it is not that, nor is it in the least like the mincing paces of a pied wagtail, which, when walking, lifts each foot like a high-stepping horse; still less is it a hop, nor is it a shuffle. Their carriage is so easy that they seem to progress without any effort.

The differences in the plumage of the Continental and British chaffinches are so slight that to differentiate them in the field must be impossible. Chaffinches ringed in Scotland and England have been recovered in Ireland, Belgium and Sweden, and others ringed in Heligoland, Holland and Belgium have turned up in England, Scotland and Ireland. A large migration eastward was reported from Skokholm, off the Pembroke Coast, in October 1937. It is possible that some continental chaffinches reach west Somerset. I always notice an increase here in autumn and have seen flocks as large as five hundred in winter. Whether these are our own residents or migrants it is impossible to state: quite probably both kinds are included.

Chaffinches rise later and roost earlier than crepuscular birds such as robins, blackbirds and thrushes. Notes kept during one winter show that they appear from twenty to twenty-five minutes later in the morning and retire about half an hour sooner at night. Compared with those of these species their eyes are small. Weather conditions naturally affect these data: chaffinches appear later and roost earlier on dull or windy mornings and evenings.

For roosting places they often choose larch or fir-woods: I know one wood partly of ilex which is a favourite dormitory. Evergreens such as laurel, laurestinus and holly are frequented and also thorn brakes and hedges. In some communal roosts males have been found to outnumber females, but in others the opposite is the case.

Little is known about the individual life histories of wild birds under natural conditions in the field, untrammelled by cages. Modern ornithology appears more and more to aim at reducing field-work to an elaborate system of census making and card indexing by teams of workers. These methods have scientific utility, but there is a danger that the bird as a living entity may in consequence be ignored. It would be lamentable if ornithology should degenerate into mere fragmentation and forget the Hegelian dogma that 'wholes are more than the arithmetical sum of their parts,' and its corollary that 'the nature of the parts is actually determined by the wholes to which they belong'. A goldfinch is more than an assembly of gold, scarlet and fawn feathers, plus a raindrop tinkle of silver notes. It is a live and vivid personality, which includes but transcends the catalogue of its physical attributes. And this is equally true of a chaffinch.

The difficulty of tracing the life history of the individual bird lies in the impossibility of accurate identification in the field. In 1932 I began trapping and ringing the birds which frequent or visit my garden. My principal object was to be able to identify them and thus to follow their life history, but I also hoped to gain information about the ages to which they attain and incidentally to learn how far my garden population was constant. The results, if they are not so far quite as satisfactory as I had anticipated, have been enlightening.

For trapping I use a wire-trap rather more than a foot long and about 6 inches wide. I bait it with food and manipulate it with a string led through my study window. When the bird is captured I cover it while in the trap with an old mackintosh and keep it in darkness while the ring is placed on its leg. By using this method the bird is less frightened, and, I believe, does not associate me with the operation. That birds do not thus suffer much inconvenience nor lose their tameness is shown from the fact that when ringed they frequently return to the trap, sometimes only a few hours after release, and that some ringed birds still take food from my hand.

Down to the end of 1942 I have ringed in this manner over a hundred chaffinches, adults or young. A few of these did not return; most of the rest were seen in or near my garden for less than a year. Of the others, nine were over two years old, and six over three years old when last seen. The hen chaffinch mentioned in the next chapter was at least seven years and three months old when she disappeared. It seems from these records that the average life of a chaffinch does not often exceed two or three years, and ringing of other smaller passerines leads me to the same conclusion. I allude to this in the chapter on bird biographies.

The rings enabled me to chronicle the doings of some of my chaffinches. Some of them nested in our garden. Others nested off the premises, but still came to our bird tables for food for their young. Two hens remained constant to us for nearly two years. One of them would come indoors. In the spring of 1937 she lost the sight of one eye and we saw no more of her after May 9th. I fear she fell a victim to a sparrow hawk which had acquired the sporting rights over this district.

I notice that many ringed chaffinches after a fairly long stay with us disappear either in spring or in autumn, and early winter. It is probable that the spring absentees find distant territories in which they mate and nest, and that the other deserters join the autumn and winter flocks and forget to revisit us, or mate next spring with visitors whose breeding territory is outside our area. Sometimes these absentees return in severe weather.

Opposite: Cock chaffinch at nest

One ringed pair, however, remained faithful to us for two seasons. They mated in April 1937 and were constantly together during that month. I had some doubts as to the constancy of the cock, for early in May he engaged in combat with an unringed male over an unringed hen. I failed to see the *dénouement*, but the suspicions aroused were unjustified, for in June I had ocular proof of his conjugal fidelity to a strictly monogamous union: later he was assiduous in conveying food to his offspring in a copse opposite our land.

Early in February 1938 the same pair began to consort together, and their association continued throughout March and April. Though I suspected that they were nesting somewhere near, it was not till the first week in May that I detected the cock, and subsequently the hen, carrying food to a nest high up in a holly just outside our garden: the site was well concealed.

In June this devoted couple again began connubial relations: they mated on the lawn in front of our windows. Cutting back the wistaria on the house a few days later I disturbed the hen from a nest containing two eggs just below my bedroom window: this unusually small clutch was successfully hatched. The couple of nestlings were again assiduously fed by the parents. I ringed the two fledglings, and for some days their parents fed them on the bird-table and in the copse opposite, but after that they disappeared and we have not seen them again.

The two old ones were always present until November 9th: after that date the hen was absent until February 5th, 1939, when she returned and began 'keeping company' with the cock again. They were constantly together till February 27th, when the hen disappeared again: On March 5th I found her dead in the garden. An autopsy revealed that she died of a fractured skull. There were also neck injuries, almost certainly caused by a bird's beak. Such injuries are usually associated with fighting: I fear that either her mate or a rival cock was responsible. Shortly afterwards her mate was accidentally killed in a trap. But for these accidents the pair would probably have mated again.

A rather curious incident which I noticed in connection with this pair was the refusal of the cock to respond to the hen's solicitation to mate while the young were being fed. In June 1942 another hen chaffinch which was, with her mate, feeding young from my bird-table, often postured sexually to the cock, and also sometimes waved her head and body from side to side as a fledgling does when being fed. Her mate made no response to her posturing except on one occasion, when he also waved his head and body. During the

Opposite: Young merlins partly fledged. Chaffinch's nest built on the top of a wren's nest

E

breeding season courtship, posturing, coition, nest building, egg-laying, brooding and feeding young form together one cycle of behaviour; actions appropriate to any one phase of that cycle may be used to express any one of the instincts which form part of it. E. Selous in *Realities of Bird Life* (p. 313) wrote that it was quite understandable that sexual excitement should find relief in any set of violent actions to which the bird is accustomed, just as the language in which a man expresses anger or surprise may have no relevancy to the particular occasion of it. As E. A. Armstrong writes in his recently published *Bird Display*: 'When birds continue habits beyond the stage in the reproductive life cycle in which they serve a useful purpose we have cyclic vestigial customs.' This hen chaffinch expressed her 'young feeding' emotion by posturing, and the cock by his head and body waving.

CHAPTER VIII

OUR TAME CHAFFINCHES

During the summer, while we have our meals on the flags outside our south windows, the chaffinches become very tame: as we feed them they walk round our feet, under the table, and occasionally perch upon it. Looking down upon a cock chaffinch from above you can distinguish every separate feather on his blue head and russet mantle, watch him turning the hemp seed with his tongue as he holds it between his horny mandibles, and hear it crack. You may note, too, that his long middle toe is slightly turned inwards, to get a good grip.

For a long time I could not induce our chaffinches to feed from my hand. Their small eyes betoken suspicion: they became wary as soon as I held my fingers level with the flags on which the crumbs were spread, though they took food only a few inches distant from my finger-ends. And the fledgling chaffinches showed the same suspicion. Was this wariness a piece of inherited instinct, or did they learn discretion from their parents' example? Such questions may seem trivial, but if we could interpret them correctly they might lead to the elucidation of some of the *arcana* of bird-behaviour. The border line between instinct and intelligence in birds and animals is a very tenuous one: it is only by careful observation of individuals that we can ever hope to discriminate; even the smallest incident properly understood may prove to be a clue of infinite importance.

No doubt some fortunate human beings are endowed with a certain magnetism which disarms the suspicions of wild birds. I can remember the man in one of the London Parks on whose arms, head and shoulders the sparrows used to perch in numbers. I once knew a lady who could put her hand beneath a sitting robin and feel the warm eggs, and another whom a brown owl allowed to take a similar liberty. These privileges are not vouchsafed to all. But anyone who can remain quiet—and does not keep a cat—can teach wild birds to trust them. And they will thus learn more of their individualities than from any cage-bound captive. A tamed bird in the bush is its natural self.

However, I found that with patience and perseverance this suspicion on the part of chaffinches could be overcome. For some seven years I enjoyed the companionship of a hen chaffinch and during the last three years our acquaintance ripened into an intimate friend-ship. I thus learned much of her life history; but the more I watched her the more I realised the difficulty of understanding the workings of a bird's embryonic mentality.

She was hatched not later than the spring or summer of 1931, for it was early in 1932 that I first noticed she was beginning to suffer from the disease known, in the domestic fowl, as 'scaly leg', a 'malady most incident' to chaffinches, but as she would never enter the trap in which I ring birds I was unable to treat it medicinally.

During 1932 and 1933 she was about our garden, though with occasional absences, but it was not until May 1934 that I began to watch her intensively.

A chaffinch's nest is one of the loveliest works of art conceived by any of our British birds: to observe its construction is a privilege. On May 24th I saw this hen chaffinch (whom, from her swollen legs we named 'Gouty') carrying minute fragments of cobweb from one of our bird-tables towards a rambler-rose pergola, about four feet high, whose top consists of a lath two to three inches broad. By evening the foundation of the nest had been neatly sketched out upon the top of the lath with morsels of moss, cobweb, hair and strands of string. The next day lichen, more moss, and hair had been added, and the day after the rim of the nest was two fingers high. As its walls rose she stood in the middle with wings and tail pointing upwards, and with her feet scratched the nesting material back behind her, afterwards arranging and preening it with her bill and smoothing it with her neck and breast. The nest was finished and the first egg laid by the evening of May 30th. She did the whole of the work, though the cock was always in close attendance. It is wonder-ful that a bird so myriad-minded, so full of inconsequent, nervous energy, should be able to concentrate so intensely on nest building and later on incubation and feeding young.

I once saw the cock with a caterpillar in his beak near the hen while she was building, but I did not actually see him feed her. Coition sometimes took place near the nest while its construction was in progress, but once when the cock attempted to mate Gouty while she was busy building she repulsed him, and a fight followed.

She had laid three eggs by the evening of June 1st and was sitting: subsequently I found that she had a clutch of four, so it seems that she began to incubate before the full clutch was completed. She was a conscientious mother, leaving the nest only for short intervals to stretch her wings and feed. I had to be away from home during the next few weeks, and so was unable to note the length of incubation, but on June 25th the last fledgling flew; this made an incubation and fledging period of 23 days.

During nearly the whole of the summer of 1935 ill-health took me away from Porlock, so that I was unable to continue my life companionship with Gouty: but in June of that year my wife found a chaffinch's nest built upon the same pergola in a similar position to the nest built by Gouty in 1934, but some forty yards further east. Since, as will be seen later, she chose the same site for her second nest in 1936, there can be little doubt that this nest was also hers. Unfortunately it was destroyed in a gale.

During the winter and early spring of 1935-6 I gradually tamed Gouty. Pine-kernels were the lure to which she responded. At first she came for them at my feet: then by slow degrees I induced her to take them from my fingers: finally she would fly to me, perch on my hand and stay there to feed for some seconds while my wife photographed her. She came regularly to our bedroom window in the morning and followed me about the garden like a dog.

Early in April 1936 I saw her making advances to a cock chaffinch. The same day while both birds were feeding on the bird-table my wife saw the cock fly down into the grass with food in his beak. Gouty came down to him and he returned to the bird-table without the food. Did he feed her? The inference is that he did. While nest building she again refused to be lured from her job by her mate's too insistent wooing.

Her nest, in a buddleia on our drive, was finished and the first egg laid on the 11th. She laid four eggs, but again began to sit when there were only three. They hatched on the 26th and the last young one flew on May 11th. (Incubation, 13 days; fledging period, 15 days.) I regret to say that her mate was a thoroughly bad husband: he took no part whatever in feeding the family, possibly from a stout belief that the nurture of babes is not a man's job: and not only did he neglect his family but he even robbed his mate of food while she was feeding their offspring. In justice to my sex I hasten to record that most cock chaffinches are good fathers.

Gouty constantly came to my hand for pine-kernels which she transferred to the maws of her insatiable bantlings. Sometimes, however, she was so ravenous that she swallowed a few kernels herself. But hunger never made her long forget her maternal duties: a short, sharp note, of a lower pitch than the usual hunger call, I am sure betokened her recollection of the needs of her offspring, for it always immediately preceded her swift return to her nest.

She was, in fact, extraordinarily tame during this period, and would stand on the edge of her nest, looking down at the nestlings, while I was only a few yards distant. I noticed that with all her broods she was scrupulous in her care for the sanitation of the nest.

Gouty took her fledglings by slow degrees into the copse opposite my gate, where I saw her judiciously supplying them with a mixed diet of green caterpillars, kernels and crumbs. By June they were able to face the dangers of prowling cats and predacious jays, for Gouty again began nest building. I suspected what was afoot when I saw her vigorously repelling the advances of a cock, who I fear was her good-for-nothing first mate: unfortunately I was never able to ring him, so that identification was doubtful. Perhaps he pleaded 'I have been faithful to thee, Cynara, in my fashion!' On June 10th I saw her with a tangle of cobwebs adhering to her beak, and afterwards tracked her to our rose pergola.

Upon the flat lath two inches broad which runs along its top, Gouty once more neatly laid the foundations of the third nest that she built in this situation, which from the chaffinch's point of view is evidently what house agents call 'eligible'; in 1934 the site was only a few yards from the present one.

From her four eggs she hatched out three chicks, the fourth egg, as is often the case in a second laying, was addled. And then came tragedy. Two mornings later the nest was empty, and magpies, rascally thieves of eggs and young, were about. There is little doubt they were the culprits. Gouty took her loss philosophically: birds, and most wild things, have little memory of pain. She still came to my hand. To receive the confidence of a wild creature is a great privilege. I know no more delightful sensation than the touch of Gouty's tiny claws upon my fingers; their grip is firm yet trustful. It is like the touch of a baby's fingers. She had some pretty ways: once, after consuming a kernel on my hand, she floated earthward, and delicately quenched her thirst with a dew-drop from a blade of grass.

During the autumn and winter of 1936, Gouty became even more docile. She would now perch on our hands and remain there for even half a minute while she consumed up to six pine-kernels, looking serenely up into our faces between whiles, and tidily picking up from our palms the minutest fragments.

A bird's principal winter occupation is the absorption of food; dusk comes at four o'clock or soon after, and from then till eight the next morning, some sixteen hours, their bodies receive no sustenance. True, their rapid digestion is then dormant, but when they wake they are ravenous. That is why Gouty and her friends appeared at our bedroom window soon after sunrise, and why

.during the next eight short hours of daylight they wasted no time in stoking up. In fact they spent most of their time on our bird-tables.

However, though it was a trying winter, with snow in six-foot drifts on the moor in January and still lying in smirched patches till Easter, spring came at last. In the second week of April 1937, when daffodils were nodding and the sight of primroses starring every hedge-bank thrilled us with joy, we noticed Gouty consorting with a cock chaffinch and ultimately accepting his advances. Whether he was her lazy husband of the previous year I cannot say definitely, but I believe he was, for again this time I never saw him help her to feed her young.

She was most secretive over her nest building; we suspected from her furtive behaviour that she had a nest: she would eye me suspiciously and then dive out of sight into the shrubbery: it was only in the first week in May that I discovered her feeding a single youngster in a nest in our macrocarpa. At the time when she must have been about to lay her eggs we had noticed that she seemed a little peevish; she refused food and stood on one leg with ruffled and dishevelled feathers; such vapours are incident to expectant motherhood.

Beside the one nestling, there were two eggs, but perhaps because of the inclement weather both were addled. As the one hungry bantling received its mother's sole attention it thrived amazingly and left the nest with a white ring on its leg when only about ten days old. But I fear its precocity was its doom, for it disappeared after a couple of days: there are prowling cats, not ours.

Gouty, with cheerful and phlegmatic optimism, at once set about raising another family. I doubt whether she was conscious of regret at the disappearance of her first. This time, I believe, she chose a different mate, a bird of smarter appearance, and, as transpired later, with a higher sense of duty. I saw her plucking strands of string from the ties of the orchard apple trees, and traced her to a half-built nest in the surrounding thorn hedge. Her new spouse followed her everywhere, encouraging her in the good work with vibrant chirruppings, though he wisely recognised that the furnishing and decoration of a nursery is a purely feminine affair.

She worked hard, aided by a plentiful diet of caterpillars, and in four days her second nest was completed and the first egg laid. This time she laid four; like a good mother she sat very closely, but now and again came out of the nest to me for food, making known her desire for my immediate attention to her wants by an imperative anxious note whose timbre bespoke both hunger and impatience to return to her domestic duties at the earliest possible moment.

The young, blind and naked, emerged from the shells in about twelve days. I am glad to be able to record that this time Gouty's mate took a man's share of the work of supplying nourishment to the family, and showed meticulous care in feeding his offspring in strict rotation. Evidently Gouty's second choice was a wise one. As her fledglings grew older she weaned them to the pine-kernel habit: it was curious to see that, when soliciting these body-building dainties from me, she waved her head and body from side to side after the manner of her own insatiable brood. At this stage she was all mother-hood.

Before these fledglings flew from the nest (on June 13th) I ringed one for identification. For some days both parents fed them about the garden, but then they disappeared.

Nearly a month later, a friend who lives half a mile away at the other end of the village, surprised at the sight of a chaffinch wearing coloured bracelets on her bird-table, rang my wife up, demanding an explanation: (being a reputed ornithologist I receive enquiries even for lost parrots!). It was the young bird recently ringed by me, but since then we have had no news of the traveller.

During the winter and spring of 1937-38 it became obvious to us that the 'scaly leg' from which Gouty was suffering was becoming worse, and was causing her discomfort and hampering her passerine movements. She would stand about on one leg, looking very forlorn, and peck the affected parts. The application of petrol is said to be a remedy, so I made several unsuccessful attempts to catch her. I also tried placing food on a platform in a bird-bath filled with petrol, in the hope that thus she might bathe her legs in the fluid. But this plan had little success.

Early in April 1938 she began nest building in the jasmine only a few yards from the kitchen windows. But it was evident that her infirmity greatly handicapped her building. After a fortnight's work the nest was still unfinished though she sometimes sat upon it. I supplied shreaded cotton and string which she utilised, but the nest still had no bottom to it. This, as I have mentioned before, is formed by the hen scratching out material from the sides of the partly finished structure: but Gouty's claws were so disabled by the disease that she was unable to perform the necessary operation. Finally I inserted cotton wool and material from an old nest and she incorporated some of it. But later I found this pulled out and discarded. No further progress was made: she had evidently given this nest up as a bad job.

During her nest building I twice saw her drive away another hen chaffinch from the vicinity of the nest. This hen chaffinch defended the breeding territory, and I have seen others do so.

Her next attempt at nesting showed considerable ingenuity, for I cannot believe that her choice of site was fortuitous. A wren had constructed what turned out to be a cock nest in a buddleia bush on our drive. About a fortnight after she had abandoned the building of her first nest, I saw her come away from the buddleia, and examination showed that she was erecting a second nest on the top of the wren's nest. As building progressed it appeared that this second attempt was a better piece of work than the former jerry-built structure. We saw her mating with a cock on May 21st and the same day her first egg was laid in the new nest: a clutch of four was completed, and incubated for thirteen days. And then came yet another tragedy. There was a gale on the night of June 6th-7th and on the morning of the latter day I found that a branch woven into the nest had, in swaying, torn out one side of the structure: the almost naked young were dead on the ground below. Had I known of the danger I could have cut off the 'envious sliver' and saved the brood.

Examination showed that the roof of the wren's nest had been appropriated for the foundation of Gouty's nest. Daylight was always visible through the bottom of her first nest and probably this was the reason that she chose a second-storey nursery, resting on the wren's substructure, when her first effort came to naught. This seems to me 'intelligent' as opposed to 'instinctive' behaviour. I have never known a similar incident.

After this catastrophe Gouty disappeared, and we feared that she had met with some misadventure, as in her crippled condition she was likely to fall a victim to any foe, feline or avian. However, rather more than a fortnight later, she reappeared, but looking very unwell. She often sat huddled up with feathers fluffed out, though at intervals she was quite lively and fed hungrily on the bird-table. I made further unsuccessful attempts to catch her and give her treatment. Throughout July and August she was present in her usual haunts on our bird-table and in the garden, but still obviously in poor health. We saw her on September 11th. After that date she disappeared, and we never saw her agin. We hope her end was merciful. Naturally, after a seven years' friendship we miss her, but it was better that a life which obviously she could no longer enjoy should be no longer protracted.

Gouty was by far the tamest chaffinch we have ever known. But there were three cock chaffinches which for some three years became increasingly friendly and visited our hands for the ever-alluring pine-kernel. They mobbed us in the garden for food, and followed not only us and our neighbours but every stranger who passed our gates. If we were away for a week or more their confidence was not impaired; they met us on the doorstep, clamouring for alms.

In bed of a morning, I would become somnolently conscious of a 'spink' from the open window. Through drowsy eyelids I descried a small form perched on the top of the casement: it was one of the three cocks. He would watch me calmly but expectantly, as I rose and procured for him his first breakfast. Complete immobility allayed his fears: he flew off with his prize, followed by the other cock, who, less tame, snatched a kernel and departed in a flurry.

The tamest of the three would sometimes perch on my hand while he disposed of three kernels on end. We called him 'William the Silent', for he did not announce his arrival, as did the others, with an impatient 'spink'. I would find him quietly waiting on the window sill. If I did not get up and attend to him he would come to me in bed. He even pressed his demands in my study; I would suddenly be conscious of his presence, perched on the back of a chair, still completely silent but expectant. One day he flew in at the south bedroom window while I was dressing and consumed kernels on the seat of the east window which had been open but was then closed: when he found it was shut he was a little worried; he hopped on to the metal fastener, and fluttered and pecked at the window-pane, but returned to his repast and eventually departed with perfect composure viâ the south window. Another day the same thing happened: this time I lured him to the open casement with a kernel and he retreated in good order.

There is also a hen chaffinch which sometimes ventures inside the bedroom, but she flies in at one window, snatches a beakful and flits out of the other. These differences in degree of tameness show how birds vary in individuality. We notice when feeding our tame chaffinches that they are far more suspicious of each other than of us; they seem nervous of being attacked by a rival while taking food from our hands. A single chaffinch will come to the hand at once, but when there is a hungry mob of half-a-dozen they bicker among themselves and are wary of pitching on our fingers, since such a position leaves them open to an assault from the rear.

In writing of chaffinches in this and the preceding chapter I have drawn almost entirely on my own personal observations, for it is by means of these alone that we can ever hope to know birds intimately.

Birds are of all animals the nearest to men
for that they take delight both in music and dance,
and gracefully schooling leisure to enliven life
wer the earlier artists.

Thus Robert Bridges. They school our leisure too, and being good artists give us inexhaustible entertainment. And when we have gained their confidence they become even nearer to us.

. . . .

Since I wrote this chapter I have received a letter from Mr. A. H. Ruston, of Huntingdon, who gives me an account of another very tame cock chaffinch. Mr. Ruston lives in a quiet part of the town, and this bird invariably flies to greet him on his way home. It often accosts him in the street, flying round his head to announce its presence and picking him out from a thronged pavement. On two occasions the bird has met him outside his business, four hundred yards or so from his home. Four times it has come to him when he has walked hatless to the letter box in the Market Place, and once it followed him to the station, three-quarters of a mile away. He has deliberately tried to mislead the bird by changes of clothing, wearing rubber soles, and changing his way of walking, but it flies straight to him. He cannot, however, persuade it to perch on his hand, though it has pecked his fingers.

CHAPTER IX

A MENDIP WOODMAN

There has lately died at the mellow age of 82 an old woodman who spent the whole of his useful life plying his craft on the Somerset Mendips. His death carries me back a long way, for I had known him for sixty years. He married my old nurse Emma, and I have always kept in touch with him and his family. I remember well, when I was a very small boy, how Jim used to come courting her at the garden gate of her mother's cottage, built of grey Mendip stone, which dated from 1750. Then it was thatched, but when last I saw it its roof was of corrugated iron, a sad decline from beauty to utilitarian cheapness and makeshift, only too typical of the spoliation of the English countryside. Their courtship must have blossomed in the late seventies of the last century, and I fear that, all innocently, I must have been much in the way, but Jim never bore any malice.

Conditions were then very different. Most of the farm labourers in those days still wore smock frocks for their work-a-day attire and hitched up their corduroy trousers with straps buckled below the knee. Many of these smocks were made of hand-woven linen and beautifully 'smocked', and embroidered. But on Sundays black broad-cloth was *de rigeur*, and curious little round black hats, with the brims turned up all round and broad black hat-bands, embroidered or embossed. Occasionally an ancient top-hat, often encircled with a crape bandeau, a left-over from the last funeral, took the place of the round hat. Those who were Methodists so attired attended a service called 'class' which took place early on Sundays, and when it was over stood about in knots discussing weather, crops and kindred subjects. Much of the corn-cutting was still done by hand and on warm August mornings a string of men and women carrying sickles would pass along the foot-path near the cottage, exchanging chaff and greetings with Emma and her mother. And I remember at least one milkmaid who sang as she carried her pails. Women, whether 'church or chapel', all curtseyed to the Parson. He was a fine Victorian type, fresh complexioned, erect and dignified, with white hair and a fringe of white whisker.

The cottage garden was small, but to my childish recollection still seems immense; a cobbled path ran down to the gate in a low wall, lichened and topped with stone-crop, and on one side of the house grew a tall damson tree, frothed with blossom in spring, and in a good year branch-bowed with fruit, not the larger and more luscious damson plums, which are now popular, but the small, hard kind, tart to the palate, like sloes, but excellent for puddings and jam. Near the gate was the well, to me a fascinating spot, for its waters were partially hooded by rough stone in whose walls grew delicate little fronds of fern and forget-me-nots; over its surface, a mirror for every vicissitude of blue sky and cloud-shadows, water-boatmen skated. Probably by now it has been condemned as insanitary by some meddlesome official, but we drank its water unboiled and were none the worse. I cannot remember many of the flowers in the garden, but I know there were some white buttons of roses and bushes of boys-love. And in the cottage windows hung pots of sweet-smelling musk, a plant which, with its secret, has vanished. Certainly its scent seems to belong more to the last century than to this, which fouls our country lanes with petrol-fumes.

The hamlet in which Emma and her mother lived could hardly be called a village: it consisted of a few scattered cottages, one or two larger houses, a church, a diminutive chapel and two inns. There were no shops, but Emma thought nothing of walking to a village some three miles distant, to do her shopping, or even to the nearest town, four or five miles away. There was only one carrier and of course no motor cars: when cottagers wanted things they had to walk and fetch them, nor in those days did it seem any hardship to have to do so. Now, tradesmen's vans go everywhere, or did until the War brought petrol rationing.

In the early eighties Jim and Emma were married, and occasionally I used to spend part of my holidays in their first little home amid fields rich with cowslips on the edge of the wood in which Jim worked. They were very poor at first. Jim once told me that he could then give Emma only ten shillings a week for household expenses! Such a sum, though it went further in the eighties than today, did not allow any luxuries. As was usual, in those days, they kept a pig. Jim made his living by making hazel-hurdles and the 'spicks' or 'spars' which are employed in thatching ricks and houses. At first he worked for a master: the rate of pay was sixpence for a bundle of a hundred spicks; as it took even as quick a worker as Jim half-an-hour to make and tie up a bundle it meant hard work to make both ends meet. The saplings and small timber in the wood were sold by auction every autumn. The first year after his marriage Jim tried with his small savings to buy a strip, but prices ranged too high, and he had to wait. However, at the next year's auction he succeeded in making his first purchase, and after that Jim was always his own master, making hurdles and spicks out of his own wood, or employing others to do so, and supplying them direct to farmers and builders.

They were a hard-working couple. Often Jim would start at daybreak for the clearing in the wood where he was cutting faggots: Emma would carry up his dinner to him later on, and when it had been eaten help him in his work, cutting twigs and knots off his 'gads' before they were tied up into faggots. Coming home in the evening they often carried heavy loads of firewood down to their cottage; their firing cost them little or nothing. From morn to night neither of them was idle.

As a boy I spent many happy hours with them in the wood especially in springtime. Oak, ash, hazel and birch were in bud, and, beneath them grew sheets of wild hyacinths, filmy blue, pale daffodils and purple orchis, while nightingale and all the woodland choir made artless music. It was Jim who showed me my first thrush's nest, in a very prickly holly, and indeed to him I owe my first lessons in the love and lore of birds which has lasted all my life. Occasionally he took a few days off to help local farmers. He was a good example of the fact, little appreciated by townsfolk, that those whom they are pleased to call 'yokels' are really skilled labourers, ready to turn their hands to any job, and much more adaptable than the 'hand' who spends a monotonous life manipulating one piece of machinery. One of Jim's accomplishments was rick-making: no one in the parish could make a better one, and his services were much in demand. I remember once when he was doing a hedging job Emma and I took his dinner up to him. It was spring-time; peewits were wheeling and crying all over the plough, and there by Jim's direction, but only after a long search, I found my first peewit's nest, and saw my first cuckoo. I could show you now, after some sixty years, the tree in which the bird pitched and called. There is another memory, less pleasant. Wishing to make closer acquaintance with some young thrushes we took a nestful of them intending to cage and feed them. They were confined in a basket and conveyed home, but when we arrived they were all dead. That cured me of trying to cage wild birds.

As I grew older I saw less of the couple, but from Emma's letters and occasional visits I gathered that times were no longer so hard with them. One summer I spent a week with them at their cottage, living their simple life as one of themselves, and thoroughly enjoying it. It was evident that they had prospered. Jim was now buying not only saplings for his hurdles but also timber which he sold to neighbouring collieries at a good profit. His son, now grown up, had a passion for horses; he looked after the hauling, carrying faggots to the spick yard and spicks and hurdles and timber to customers.

They both still worked as hard as ever. When engaged on a job at home Jim rose at five or six in the morning; he took a frugal breakfast of tea and bread and butter, though there was plenty of bacon and fresh eggs from his own fowls if he wanted them. He would be busy with his hurdles or spicks till one o'clock when he made a good dinner of meat and vegetables, but never took any pudding and rarely touched ale or cider. But this meal took him only a few minutes— 'You won't mind if I do get back to my work'—and off he would go to ply his craft till teatime, bread and butter with a strawberry or two from his garden. After tea, still more work, and in the cool of the evening a row of potatoes hoed or some small garden job. Bread and cheese, or perhaps a slice of cold meat for supper. Emma's day was quite as busy; besides helping Jim to 'shirp' knots off his gads she seemed always either to be preparing the next meal or clearing up the remnants of the last, for her son never knew when his carting would bring him home and he usually arrived hungry. She swept out the cottage and dusted every article and innumerable china ornaments—'a lot of little caddles', she called them—at least once a day, and in her spare time she and her daughter brushed and mended the men's clothes and did the household washing and ironing. By half-past nine all the family was in bed. A well-spent day for all of them.

At his own trade of hurdle- and spick-making Jim was an expert. I can see him now sitting at work in the little shanty in a corner of his garden, clothed in shirt and corduroys and thick boots, his face, neck, hands and arms tanned a rich brown by years of exposure to all weathers. At his side was a bundle of 'gads' (saplings from which the twigs and knots had been removed) cut to a length of about five feet. Lifting one of them from the ground with his hook and laying it across his knees, he sliced off the lower end, leaving a clean slanting surface. A vertical blow on this surface split the gad at one end. Inserting his hook in this cleft, he gradually worked it down the gad with a jolly crackling noise, until, as he reached the lower end, it fell divided into two halves. Each of these halves was then split in the same manner until every gad in the bundle had been shaped into four slim lengths of lissom wood. These he trimmed carefully and pointed bluntly at each end. He then selected a piece of withy or hazel cut so thin that he could curve and plait it into a circlet about 9 inches in diameter. Into this circlet he fitted a couple of stouter strips of wood, intersecting cross-wise in the middle of the ring so as to divide it into four equal segments. This he placed upright on the ground. Next, taking one of the four lengths into which the gads had been divided, he deftly twisted and doubled it into the shape of a hairpin, and placed its two pointed ends in one of the segments of the wooden circle. The 'hairpin' automatically tried to straighten itself out again, but was kept in place by the rim of the circlet and the cross-wise pieces. More spicks were inserted in the same manner until all the segments were filled and a bundle of one hundred was made up. The cross sticks were then withdrawn and the wooden circlet formed a firm girdle round the slim Victorian waist of the bundle. A deft piece of craftmanship.

Spick-making is, indeed, a fine art. Jim, was an artist at his trade. As you watched him cleverly turning the gad on his knees, chopping and splitting and shaping it, with a litter of curly white shavings gathering round his feet, you would think that no-one could do the work more neatly. He seemed a past master of his craft. But he told me that his father was an even better workman and was the finest spick-maker he ever saw. It was good, too, to watch him at hurdle-making; to mark how cleverly he wove the hazel-wands through and round the uprights, pressing them down firmly with the heel of his boot and thus building up compact and windproof hurdles which made admirable fences and shelters for sheep folds.

The actual making of spicks and hurdles was, of course, only a part of the trade. In winter the wood had to be cut, tied into faggots and stacked upright against trees until it could be carted down to the shanty which formed the workshop. Carting was also an important branch of his business for customers were scattered, all over the countryside. It was wonderful to see what a load could be stacked upon one of his dillies, carts rather like hay waggons. At the bottom were placed a dozen bundles of faggots, and then upon this foundation were piled bundles of spicks, one after another, till the load rose some fifteen feet from the ground, the weight being concentrated towards the front of the dilly. The load was secured by two chains, one passed athwart the front and the other athwart the back of the pile. Then two stout stakes were driven down into the wood from the top. Round these stakes the chains were twisted by means of a wooden bar, used as a tourniquet, until the whole stack was compressed into a compact mass which no jolt on the road could dislodge.

Opposite: Nuthatch. This plate should be looked at vertically as the bird is climbing the tree

This primitive craft must be of great antiquity. Here, in a corner of England where in the course of centuries there had been less change than in more populated districts, there survived an industry that was carried on practically in the same way and with the same primitive implements as in the Middle Ages. The hook and the axe were the only steel tools that the woodman used and their shape has not changed materially for hundreds of years. His only other implements were his strong quick hands, his stout arms, and, when hurdle-making, his boot-heel. Like all skilled trades it has its mysteries, handed down from generation to generation.

I like best to think of Jim as he was in his early fifties; he was then still in the prime of life. Though a Somerset man born and bred, his ancestry was, I believe, Welsh, for he was of that Iberian type, thickset and sturdy, with dark-brown hair and eyes, broad brows, square-cut face and features which I have seen in Pembrokeshire. His profile always reminded me of Holbein's picture of Erasmus. The strip of side-whisker which alone was allowed to grow on his clean-shaven face was then a little grey. Little wrinkles ran up to his eyes, brown as a still pool in a hazel-shaded Mendip stream; they had that tranquil, inward look which comes of a life spent alone with nature, and were as young as they had been thirty years before. As he paused in his work to tell me one of the many wonderful things which he had noticed during half a century of life in the woods, they seemed to look not only into but through and beyond mine. They could twinkle, too, on occasion, when he told a tale of his younger days. Now he snared rabbits in his own paddock, but I suspect the art was learned elsewhere. A rabbit awakes all a countryman's sporting instincts. I remember joining Jim and Emma in a rabbit hunt on a Sunday evening's walk. Emma used her then ample skirts as an improvised stop, but the rabbit eluded them, and us.

Though so fine a craftsman Jim was what our town-minded educationists would call illiterate. He could not read and his penmanship progressed no further than a sprawling signature. But, in compensation, his memory was extraordinarily accurate. He would come in of an evening after his day's work away and reel off to Emma a long list of orders for hurdles or other material which he had picked up on his way home, and she would commit them to writing. He and Emma had been 'butties', i.e. chums, at the village school together, but he was one of a long and needy family, and his father took him away from school at the age of six to help in his work; thus he often had no more than two days' schooling in the week. But Emma was a good scholar; she, and later his son and daughter, kept

Opposite: Young cuckoo

F

his accounts and attended to his correspondence. He talked the broadest Somerset and still used the antique 'houzen' and 'plazen' as plurals of 'house' and 'place'.

When they had been married some thirty years Emma died after only a day's illness. Jim was never quite the same again. They were a devoted and harmonious couple: I can see them now, after many years of happy married life, sitting together hand in hand after tea on the settle in their cottage kitchen. They had a store of little intimate and personal jokes, and were always poking sly fun at one another. I never knew a happier pair.

Soon after she died he moved into a small farm with his son (now married) and his wife and an unmarried daughter. It comprised some fifty acres, chiefly pasture, with some useful sheds and linhays; he bought a few cows and the household must have been almost self-supporting. He still worked hard at his woodman's trade, but now allowed himself occasional relaxations. When I called to see him once I found him busy with his hurdles. After a few minutes' chat he suggested a walk round. I objected that I mustn't take him off his job, but his reply was: 'Oh, I've got enough saved up for to kip (i.e. keep) I'. Certainly he had earned his independence.

Though of late years I did not often see him, I know from his daughter's letters that he enjoyed a serene and happy old age, well tended by his women-folk. He made a good end, and they buried him, as he wished, beside his wife.

Though they both came of humble stock, comparative affluence never spoiled Jim and Emma. Few people can 'stand corn', but they could. They had a proper pride, strong and deep. They did not envy 'the gentry', yet they respected the old families and showed genuine regret and sympathy, when, as so often happens, they had fallen upon evil times. But the *nouveau riche* got short shrift. 'I don't think he can really be a gentleman,' remarked Emma, after relating a *gaucherie* perpetrated by one of that kind.

To some, perhaps, this may seem a chronicle of small importance. But I think it a fine record and worth relating. Here was a man, 'uneducated'—in the urban sense—who started life with nothing, and made good. Nothing? Nothing but his own grit and character! It was that and the help and encouragement of his splendid wife, which enabled him to rise from poverty—and in those days there was no 'dole'—and attain to a position still humble, perhaps, but honourable, and win the love and respect of everyone who knew him. He lived on the land and made a living out of it, and wanted nothing better. One evening at sunset he and I were leaning over the wall at the bottom of his garden, looking out over pasture and hedge-row to the distant wooded Mendips. After a silence he suddenly broke out with 'What can 'ee want better than this?' There spoke the real countryman; he loved the land and loved it in a way no week-ending townsman can understand; it was part of his being. Such men are natural gentlemen.

CHAPTER X

BIRD BEHAVIOUR: ROUTINE AND
INTELLIGENCE

The observations recorded in this chapter (most of which were made in my own garden) and my comments upon them cover little or nothing not already well known to the hard-boiled ornithologist. To him it may well seem that further discussion is superfluous. But this book is not primarily written for ornithologists, but rather for those whom Miss Phyllis Bond, in her fascinating but too modest little book *Watching Wild Life*, calls 'just people', the man or woman who enjoys birds and is ready to gossip about them and their ways even if such small talk has little scientific value.

Every bird-watcher is aware that birds are in many respects the slaves of routine. The subject has been elaborated by Edmund Selous, Eliot Howard, and others. I have mentioned in a previous chapter a cock and hen chaffinch, which came to our hands for pine-kernels. Our intimate companionship with these birds gave us glimpses into their minds; their behaviour supplied instances of how much bird behaviour is a matter of routine: it conforms to a pattern. The hen chaffinch learned only by slow degrees to perch on my hand for food; first I threw down kernels for her at my feet: gradually I reduced the interval between us: then she would take them from my fingers when spread level with the ground: finally she ventured to fly up to my hand; then she stood there and fed and knew that she could do so safely. It took a long time to break down the 'fear of man' pattern of conduct.

With the cock chaffinch the process was still more protracted. He began coming to my bedroom window in the morning, and by easy stages I trained him to take a kernel from the tips of my fingers. One morning I placed the nut a little way back towards the palm of my hand; he hesitated, and half pecked at it, but did not take it. Then he pecked at my finger tips where previously I had always held the kernel. In the end he snatched the dainty when I moved it nearer to the ends of my fingers, but he would not then come on my hand.

I have set down this incident in detail because it illustrates well how bird behaviour follows a pattern. A humanistic interpretation of the cock chaffinch's pecking at the place on my fingers where the kernel was usually to be found would be that he was asking me to put the nut there. The true explanation is that he could not yet deviate from the pattern; his little mind was unable then to reach beyond it. It is only by slow steps that a bird learns to break away from routine. This chaffinch later learned to fly to and perch on my fingers for food, but it took him some weeks longer to learn his lesson; finally he perched a second or two on my fingers while consuming the kernels, but still not as long as the hen chaffinch did.

There is still one cock chaffinch which feeds from my hand and some half-a-dozen of both sexes which are almost tame enough to do so, but none of these can, so far, overcome their distrust. They cannot get out of the groove. And neither cock nor hen chaffinches will take kernels from my gloved hand. To do so would be departure from the old routine.

Nuthatches which at one time came tamely to the fence by the kitchen windows and to our bird-tables occasionally swallowed crumbs as they fed there, but more often they took these fragments to the elm which was their usual anvil for nuts, and wedged them into cracks before eating them. This is yet another example of the slavery of birds to habit. It also shows lack of intelligence, for if a nuthatch must have a crack in which to wedge his food there are plenty of suitable ones in the bark surrounding the bird-table, and journeys to the elm and back would be spared.

Birds when feeding young in the nest often adopt one line of approach and keep to it. A pair of cirl buntings one year nested, as they often do, in our macrocarpa hedge: I watched them feeding the partly fledged young and noticed that both cock and hen always flew into the macrocarpa a little to the right of the nest and then hopped through the foliage to it. A pair of lesser spotted woodpeckers feeding young were less stereotyped in their behaviour; usually the cock pitched to the right of and below the nesting hole and sidled up to it, and the hen approached in a similar manner from the left. Only once the cock took the left-hand route. These are further instances of birds' slavery to habit.

It requires something in the nature of a cataclysm, from the avian standpoint, to make a bird alter a habit once formed. Such a catastrophe is the failure of the food supply. In January 1933, after continuous hard frost for several days, gulls, blackheaded, common and herring, which had previously found food by following the plough, came down and fed on soaked crusts which we had spread on the lawn only a few yards from the windows: they squabbled vociferously among themselves. At first they were very wary, but after they had fed for some time some of the blackheaded gulls rested on the lawn:

one ate two decayed mice and a shrew, killed in my traps; cold and hunger had changed their habits.

An instance of the persistence of a habit once formed was supplied by one of a pair of spotted flycatchers which nested in a box on our house. One of the fledged young ones on leaving the nest settled upon the lawn, where the parents fed him, and on one occasion one of the old birds, after feeding him, removed the excrement. That this piece of routine behaviour should be still followed when the young bird had left the nest shows how a habit once formed may be continued after it has ceased to have any useful purpose.

This leads on naturally to the question of intelligence, or the lack of it, in birds. Most bird behaviour is instinctive, very little intelligent, and probably none is prompted by reason, using the word in the behaviourist sense.

On Dawlish Warren I once watched an immature herring gull pecking at a mussel, a common enough sight. Failing to pierce the shell it rose in the air, and giving the mollusc a toss, dropped it to the ground; though the bird made several attempts it was not successful in breaking the shell. Little or no intelligence was shown in choosing the substance on which the shell would fall: once or twice the mussel struck stones in falling, but on other occasions it pitched on sand or in the sea. There was no evidence of the gull learning by trial and error: the object was dropped fortuitously. Carrion crows and rooks use the same methods, and from the legend of the death of Aeschylus it appears that eagles show a similar lack of intelligence, though if the tortoise had struck the head of some modern poet the result might have been more satisfactory—either for the bird or the public.

I was awakened from semi-somnolence one afternoon by a hammering so loud that I thought someone was knocking at the front door. But there was no one on the doorstep; a great tit was pecking at one of the windows on the landing, apparently in the hopes of getting at a sleepy fly on the other side: hence the tattoo. A nuthatch once pecked at the glass of my study window in the endeavour to reach nuts in a matchbox inside. The failure of birds to realise that glass is impermeable shows a curious want of intelligence. And the same is true of the repeated attacks made, for instance, by chaffinches and blackbirds on the imaginary enemy reflected in a window pane.

In 1931 a pair of cirl buntings nested in our macrocarpa hedge: two youngsters hatched out, but two addled eggs remained in the nest. The two fledglings fluttered out of the nest when I approached it. Fearing that they were too young to embark upon a troublesome world, I caught one and replaced it in the nest; the other I could not find. When I returned to the nest after an interval I was surprised to find no young ones in it, but the hen brooding the two addled eggs, and this although the food calls of the young birds, who were evidently somewhere about in the hedge, were audible. I should have supposed that the cries of the fledglings, which usually make so strong an appeal to the parents, would have prevailed over the instinct to brood. The aberration was only temporary, for later in the day the nest, and its unfertile contents, were deserted, and both parents were very busy providing food for their offspring. But the incident implies lack of intelligence in the hen cirl bunting and also absence of any instinct telling her that the two eggs were addled. The 'brooding' routine was, for the time being, stronger than the response to the 'food' cries of the fledglings.

I have given an instance earlier in this chapter which seemed to argue lack of intelligence in nuthatches. But in other ways they show considerable *savoir faire*. At one time a pair became tame enough to take nuts from my wife's fingers through our windows, so we have had considerable opportunities of observing their behaviour. They seem more competent than such species as the great spotted wood-pecker to resist the invasion of their nesting holes by starlings: they plaster mud round the circumference of a hole if it is too large for their purpose; this enables them to keep avian intruders in their proper place. The plastering habit is by now instinctive, but origi-nally it may have been intelligent. A friend told my wife of an experience which shows that the nuthatch has other methods of protecting his home. The hole chosen by one pair was near the junction of a horizontal branch with the main trunk of the tree; a starling coveted this desirable residence, though the aperture was only large enough to admit his head: the nuthatch took up a strategical position on the branch, and waited there until the starling's head was in the hole: then he rained blows from above upon his enemy's shoulders, and by this means eventually drove him away. When you watch a nuthatch putting the whole force of his sturdy frame into the pick-axeing of a tough nut, you can un-derstand why even the pushful and persistent starling deemed it wiser to accept the inevitable and retire. This nuthatch's home was his castle. And his method of repelling the invader exhibited an intelligent ability to deal with an unexpected situation.

I once saw a nuthatch dislodge a nut from our fence, carry it to a notch in an elm, some forty feet up, and get to work upon it with such vigour that the nut was displaced and fell. Before it reached the ground the bird caught it in its beak, carried it to a place higher up the tree and resumed its blacksmith's task. The feat again revealed a surprising agility of both body and mind in dealing with the un-expected.

The old nuthatches carried off monkey nuts to the elm and wedged them into the cracks in the bark while they extracted the kernels. The young ones did not seem to know at first how to deal with unshelled nuts: they were unable to fix them firmly into an anvil; they pecked at them when lying loose upon the ground and often abandoned the attempt to dislodge the kernels. Shelled nuts they dealt with in the usual way. But they showed intelligence also. I wedged a monkey nut into a hole in the floor of a bird-table: a young nuthatch tried but failed to dislodge it from above: it then craned over the side of the table, knocked the nut upwards out of the hole and carried it off. A nut, intended for tits, was suspended by means of wire from a tree not far from our windows. A young nuthatch hovered in the air opposite the nut and tried to detach it with its bill; having failed twice in the attempt, it clung to the wire below the nut and succeeded in extracting it. I have seen a rook haul up a piece of fat suspended by string and devour it and Mr. John Kearton has recorded a similar piece of ingenuity on the part of a great tit.

A pair of lesser spotted woodpeckers visit a fence of split larch poles near our house in search of grubs. One morning while the cock was thus engaged a heavy shower of rain and hail came on. He flew from the fence to the post which supports a bird-table, climbed up almost to the top and hung underneath the tray on the lee side of the post till the storm was over, when he returned to the fence. To shelter thus under the umbrella showed adaptive intelligence.

In my previous book *The Lure of Birdwatching* I discussed the subject of nestlings and thirst, and said that I did not see that it would be impossible for parent birds to carry water to young in the nest, but that there was then no evidence that they did so. Since that book was published I have read Messrs. Gilbert and Brook's *Watchings and Wanderings Among Birds* in which they describe how they saw a female stork fill herself up with water from a pond close by her nest and then return and bring all the water up again, pouring it over her nestlings, who opened their beaks and caught as much of it as they could. Mr. Oliver Pike has mentioned that he saw ravens bring water to their young who were suffering from heat, and I have seen grey wagtails dip food in water before supplying it to their nestlings.

The instances cited above clearly show that water is sometimes so carried: I suspect that the practice is more general than is usually supposed. Such behaviour is surely intelligent.

The subject of intelligence leads naturally to another question which recurs to me from time to time. Can birds count?

In the summer of 1935 I was laid up with influenza. The tedium was relieved by the attentions of a very tame robin. For some time she had been in the habit of coming to our windows for sultanas, which she evidently conveyed to her young; she would pitch on the sill outside, stand on her toes and crane her head upwards until she could see if there was a prospect of food inside. El Greco, had he ever painted a robin, would have depicted it in this attitude. When I took to my bed she began to pay me regular visits. I kept sultanas in a small tin box at my bedside. She would fly in at the casement window, pitch on the bedrail, cock an expectant eye at me, and advance over the coverlet. At first she used to take the dainties from between my finger and thumb; then she learned to pitch on my hand, and finally I trained her to perch on my thumb and search for the sultanas in my palm. She was 'house trained' in her habits; in fact, her bedside manner was perfect. One morning when it was just light my wife found her on the pillow a few inches from her face.

Sometimes she swallowed one sultana herself, but more often she held the first in her beak and waited impatiently for me to give her a second, which she would tuck between the tips of her bill, and then dive for the window.

This behaviour made me wonder whether robins can count. Mr. J. G. Renier in his charming book *A Tale of Two Robins*, says that robins can count, at any rate up to two. One of his robins, called 'Robin Eagle', came to two different persons, 'Mr. Gerard' and 'Joy' for worms. If one of them was indoors and the other in the garden, he would come first to one and then to the other for worms: but if both were in the garden he did not visit the house. Also, if either Mr. Gerard or Joy and a visitor, i.e. two people only, were in the house, the robin would come for worms as boldly as if Mr. Gerard and Joy were there: but if there were visitors with them, i.e. more than two people, he held back. Mr. Renier deduced from this that Robin Eagle could count 'one, two, more', and he did not like 'more'. When one person was in the garden there must be number two in the house; when there were two either in the garden or in the house there was none in the other place. 'One, two' was right. 'More' was unusual and therefore wrong.

A neighbour of mine at one time fed a song thrush which always took four nuts or kernels in its beak, and not more. If only three were offered it waited for a fourth.

I am not convinced that these instances prove that robins or thrushes can count: for a mental act to be correctly called 'counting' there must be conscious enumeration. I believe that the robin and thrush simply took as many objects as their beaks could hold: they had no conception of number. And Mr. Renier's robin was merely made nervous by the presence of 'more' people. That is not enumeration.

Miss Frances Pitt, in *The Naturalist on the Prowl*, says that birds, with the possible exception of individual crows and ravens, are unable to count. They may distinguish between one and many, but if two persons go to a hide and one goes away, they never notice the difference, and are contented.

There are, however, two recorded observations by well-known and accurate field naturalists which carry us further than the preceding instances. Mr. Seton Gordon, in his book *Thirty Years of Nature Photography*, says that the grey or hooded crow is one of the very few birds able to count. He and his wife were photographing a nest of this species in the Outer Hebrides; the nest was on an island in a fresh-water loch; they put up a hide and employed the usual photographer's ruse, i.e. Mrs. Gordon saw her husband into the hide and rowed back to the mainland; but the old birds would not return to the nest although it contained a noisy and hungry youngster: this happened on two occasions. The next day Mr. Gordon, after seeing his wife into the hide, rigged up two dummy figures in the stern of the boat and rowed away. The crows returned at once. I have read somewhere of a similar experience with carrion crows, but cannot turn up the reference.

In *Sea Terns or Sea Swallows*, by George and Anne Marples, there is another record. In order to test the ability of a bird to recognise the nesting site, and discover whether the environmental features acted as landmarks and guides, all conspicuous objects were removed from around the nest of a little tern, and the eggs were covered completely with sand. The bird, on her second return, dropped directly on to the sand covering the nest, discovered one egg, moved it away from the nest, holding it between her beak and breast, and brooded it; then she ran across the nest site and back to the egg, brooded it again, and dragged it a little further away as before. Then again she walked over and past the nest site; she returned, found another egg, which she moved in the same manner as the first, but not so far. Then she dragged the first egg to the second and brooded them. Next she revisited the nest site, found the third egg, dragged the other two eggs to it, and finally remade the 'nest' on the old site and sat on all three eggs.

Mr. Seton Gordon's episode seems to mean that the grey crows were at any rate conscious of the difference between one and two; similarly Mr. and Mrs. Marples' tern was aware of the distinction between one and two, and two and three. If this is not quite conscious enumeration, it is something very near it.

How far have birds any sense of time? Obviously they are not conscious of its arbitrary divisions devised by mankind: still less are they conscious of absolute time in the metaphysical sense. Inasmuch as they wake and go to roost more or less at dusk and dawn they must to that extent be aware of the passage of time. It is in moments of intense absorption or emotion that for us time passes most quickly: it is then that we arrive most closely to Bergsonian 'intuition' of Duration. Birds, especially the smaller *passeres*, live intensely; they are ever alert and active, full of nervous excitement. Their hearts beat more quickly, their temperature is higher than ours. Time for them must surely pass very rapidly; short as their lives, in most cases, actually are, to birds they must seem even shorter.

CHAPTER XI

SOME BIRD PROBLEMS

That birds, like human beings, have well-marked individualities, traits of character that distinguish them from their fellows, is well known to field naturalists and bird lovers. But most bird-books with which I am acquainted have little to say about the subject, though its fascination is unlimited. Many of the problems discussed in this chapter are suggested by my own observations on Exmoor and the neighbouring countryside. There is no need to go far afield: the commonest birds supply plenty of unsolved problems if the mind is alert.

Mr. Ian M. Thompson, in his book *Birds from the Hide*, which contains some very fine bird-photographs, makes some interesting observations on the varying individualities of birds of the same species: one pair of great-crested grebes was so tame that the female not only refused to leave the nest when his boat approached, but screamed at and pecked him; all the other pairs nesting in the same water were suspicious. Some bearded tits were not at all timid at the nest, but of other pairs sometimes the cock and sometime the hen was the more easily alarmed. Everyone who has watched birds intensively must have noticed the same thing: you can tame some robins to feed from your hand with little difficulty: others will never come. An old cock greenfinch, 'grandfather', which feeds daily on our bird-table drives off all intruders. Others are more pacific. One starling on the same table allowed a greenfinch to drive him off; another starling treated the aggressor with absolute indifference and took no notice of its hissing at him, but went on quietly feeding. Most buzzards when their nest is approached sheer off and mew at the intruder from a distance. Others threaten attack; I have known them fly straight at my head and throw up only at a few yards distance. A robin and dunnock, both identifiable by coloured rings, are, as my German master used to say, 'at blockheads together': the robin simply cannot stand the sight of the dunnock and drives it off venomously as soon as it appears on or near the bird-table. A song thrush visitor to our tables wore his head feathers so fluffed out that we called him 'the buffle-headed thrush': he looked the part: his expression was vacuous, and he was so stupid that he once allowed a vulgar and pushful sparrow to turn him out of the bird-bath. A 'village idiot' among birds!

When I flush a flock of lapwings, often the bulk of the concourse flies in one direction, but a smaller party departs in another, apparently following a leader. The same thing happens with the immense hordes of golden plover that in winter haunt the shore near Minehead and the higher portions of Exmoor. Sometimes when the congregation has taken to wing a single bird remains and eventually flies off in a different direction. Is this individual a sluggard or a pariah? A lonely coombe near Porlock was at one time inhabited by one cock blackbird, and one robin, and one only. Why, when all the fertile fields and copses of the valley were available, did these birds choose this solitary and remote existence? Territory, perhaps, but why such a territory? There must have been some individual preference. If it were possible to distinguish particular birds in the field I believe it would be found that they vary as much in individuality as human beings. My experiments with birds ringed with coloured rings have, so far as they extend, confirmed me in this opinion.

The question whether birds pair for life is a difficult one. But the presence of pairs of the same species in winter has long suggested to me that some of them do so. All one winter one pair, and one only, of marsh tits, cole tits, great tits, pied wagtails and nuthatches fed on our bird tables. I suspect strongly—but prefer not to be more dogmatic—that these pairs were life partnerships. Nuthatches especially are companionable little birds: I have seen them in pairs in every month of the year.

As to birds which flock together in winter, it is impossible to say whether pairs keep together, but when, early in the year, the schools of long-tailed tits break up into couples I wonder whether the individuals may not have remained attached to each other all the time, though to our eyes all seemed to be inextricably mixed.

I have found male and female of many other species together, in winter, and always near the same spot. For instance, I always know where to find pairs of stonechats on certain places on the moor, and the same applies to dippers in suitable localities. I have also found two wrens and two goldfinches in each other's company out of the breeding season; two wrens nested in the eaves of my tool-shed one winter. Male and female of both these species are alike in plumage, so the birds may not have been a pair, but goldfinches with us are usually in bevies of from half-a-dozen to twenty in winter.

Absolute proof can only be obtained by the trapping and ringing of various species over a long period. My own observations on this head do not, so far, justify dogmatism. But the case of the pair of ringed chaffinches which mated and reared three successive broods, referred to in a previous chapter, is significant. The same pair of ringed blue tits mated and nested in different boxes in my garden in 1939 and 1940. These birds kept together throughout the summer, autumn and winter of 1939 and up to July 1940, when the hen disappeared. The cock remained until November 1940. Another pair which nested in my garden in 1942 has been constantly on my bird-tables down to the end of that year.

Popular opinion holds that birds begin to mate on St. Valentine's Day: really many are paired long before this. Watching the mating of birds, I have often wondered what actually it means to them. Is there not sometimes more in it than mere instinctive, physical attraction? Coition is, in some species, e.g. great spotted woodpeckers, followed by caressing with the bill, and many males feed the hen before and during incubation of the eggs. If, as I believe, some birds pair for life, there must be some bond more lasting than the physical attraction manifested in mating time. In course of ages will birds reach an even higher plane, or is their behaviour stereotyped in this as in many other respects?

At intervals newspaper correspondence recurs about the alleged hibernation of cuckoos. In that quaint old book, Ray's edition of *Willughby's Ornithology*, published 1687, there are two curious stories relating to this. According to one of these a Zurich countryman, having laid a log on the fire in winter, heard a 'cuckow' cry in it.

The other story tells how when some servants cast some old rotten willows into a furnace they heard 'a "cuckow" singing three times'. On the willow being pulled out of the fire and cut open, they drew out first 'meer feathers' but later a living cuckoo entirely bare of plumage; it was said to have lived two years.

Bewick, in his Introduction to his *History of British Birds* (1797 Edition) relates how a few years previously a young cuckoo was found in the thickest part of 'a close whin bush'; when taken out it was alive, but, like the one mentioned above, 'quite destitute of feathers'. Being kept warm and carefully fed, it grew fresh plumage; the next spring it escaped, and flying away, gave its usual call.

In 1923 a correspondent in the *Morning Post* mentioned a young cuckoo being found in the case of a grandfather (not a 'cuckoo') clock in a Shropshire farmhouse. Placed in front of the fire, it woke up, bawled cuckoo once, and so died.

In my press-cutting book I find four other similar cases: dates are unfortunately not noted, but the first two were published in *Country Life*. A cuckoo, caught in summer and kept as a pet, mysteriously disappeared in early winter. In January it was found inside an old boot in a cupboard, quite naked, but surrounded by its moulted feathers. It was alive but sluggish. The second was discovered in winter by a builder, when pulling down an old wall, in a hole in the brickwork. It was in exactly the same condition as the bird found in the boot. The third was uncovered by a stonemason, when demolishing an ancient cottage, in an old nest under the eaves; it, too, was covered by its own shed feathers. The fourth was a cuckoo reared and kept in a cage. It disappeared at the end of the summer: later the owner found that the bird had buried itself in the old straw at the bottom of the cage; it also was covered with its own discarded feathers. The two last-mentioned cuckoos both died within half an hour of being exposed.

I myself was told a similar story by a Somerset man some twenty-five years ago. He was carting stone from a quarry in November, and saw the quarrymen unearth a live cuckoo curled up in a ball in a cavity in the rock. There seemed to be a kind of film over its eyes, and here again, when handled all its feathers came off.

I do not suppose that any of the birds mentioned in these stories were really hibernating, i.e. sleeping out the winter. I suspect that they were late-hatched young cuckoos; it is a pity that the feathers were not preserved in any instance so that this might be ascertained. When overtaken by the cold they would crawl into shelter. If undiscovered they would not have survived. The fact that their feathers came out points to a very low state of animation.

It is strange how facts about birds which seem obvious when discovered can be overlooked even by those whose knowledge of wild life is extensive. The woodcock is a bird which has for hundreds of years been a favourite quarry with sportsmen. Yet it is little more than thirty years ago since my friend, the late Mr. Charles Whymper, the well-known artist, antiquarian and naturalist who lived at Houghton, near St. Ives, Huntingdon, first discovered the curious position of the woodcock's ear. (See diagram on p. 96.) While shooting in 1907 he killed a woodcock: his man who picked the bird up, remarked at the 'great hole in his skull'. Mr. Whymper, on examining the bird, saw at once that this hole was the ear, and that it was *in front of* the eye. (See No. 1 in diagram.) As he could find no reference to this peculiarity in ornithological works, he took the bird to Mr. W. P. Pycraft at the British Museum, who subsequently wrote in *The Field* for May 18th, 1907:—

'My friend Mr. C. Whymper has recently drawn my attention to a curious point in the anatomy of the woodcock, which I think should be placed on record, and to his credit, for the discovery is his. This point concerns the position of the external aperture of the ear, which is remarkable in that it is placed immediately in front of the eye. In the common snipe this aperture lies beneath the eye, while in *all* other birds it lies behind the eye.' (See No. 2 in diagram.)

In *The British Bird Book*, published in 1910 (Vol. III, pp. 285-6), Mr. Pycraft writes: 'Snipe and woodcock stand alone among birds in respect of the extreme shortening of the base of the skull, which

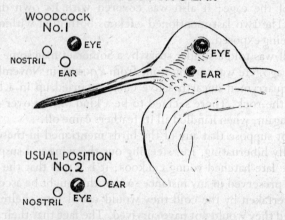

THE WOODCOCK'S EAR

WOODCOCK No. 1

NOSTRIL   O
O   EYE
O   EAR

EYE

EAR

USUAL POSITION No. 2

NOSTRIL   O
O   EYE
O   EAR

has tilted the floor upwards, so that the cerebrum (i.e. the brain) instead of lying in front of the cerebellum, lies above it, or, in other words, the long axis of the brain, instead of running parallel with the long axis of the skull, runs at right angles to it. This bending downwards and forwards of the brain cavity has been attended by a shifting forwards of the aperture of the ear.' He adds that in the snipe the aperture of the ear is under the eye, but in the woodcock it has shifted still farther forwards, so that it is in front of the eye.

In his book *Birds of Great Britain*, p. 147, Mr. Pycraft also writes on the same subject:—

'The explanation is interesting and forms a striking illustration of the effects of "use" which is, even now, denied by some as a factor in evolution. It is a matter of common knowledge that these birds' (i.e. snipe and woodcock) 'obtain much of their food by probing in soft ground for worms, and this . . . has brought about a "telescoping" of the base of the skull, which has brought the auditory region, in consequence, far forward; so that it has shifted through nearly half a circle.'

Opposite: Cock stonechat

The diagram on p. 96 is adapted from a painting by Mr. Whymper.

When one considers the wastage in nestling birds, both in the nest and after they have left it, from cats, hawks, weasels, stoats, jays, magpies and, sometimes, little owls, it is easy to understand why species which have two or even three broods in a season do not increase. But when once a bird reaches the adult stage its chances of survival are greater and that even if it is maimed by some misadventure. The jackdaw with injured mandibles, mentioned in *Wild Exmoor*, survived for over two years, and a hen blackbird which had lost half of her upper mandible haunted our garden and bird-tables for a similar period. But it is significant that both these birds disappeared after cold spells; lowered vitality had weakened them. Darkness, with lowered temperature, probably numbed them into insensibility, a merciful death.

Mr. William Beebe, the American naturalist, in his book *Nonsuch, Land of Water*, quotes two curious instances of the survival of maimed birds. He recognised on one of the Bermuda Islands a turnstone bereft of the right foot and lower part of the leg, for three years in succession, and another turnstone with a deformed right foot for two successive years. The Bermudas are nearly 700 miles from New York and 850 from St. Thomas, an island in the West Indies, which are approximately the nearest land to north and south. That birds so injured should travel such distances and survive is even more amazing. Mr. Beebe noticed that when searching for food its companions, though quarrelsome among themselves, gave way to the first cripple.

If a bird is so maimed as to make the chances of recovery remote, the most merciful course is to end its life at once. But if there is a fair chance of its convalescence it should be confined in some place where it can be fed and protected from its enemies. The wire cage which covers our small fruit we frequently use as a hospital. A hen chaffinch with an injured wing, which I rescued from the roadside, made a complete cure in this hospice in seven weeks, and flew away quite happily when released. But a sheld-duck, which I found with a wounded pinion and a broken leg on Porlock Marsh and carried under my arm to the same refuge, refused food, and was so miserable that I had to despatch it—a hateful job.

No doubt many of these injuries to birds are caused by those break-neck traps which are set to catch mice in gardens. It is, of course, necessary to keep down these pests, but the old-fashioned box mouse-traps are equally effective and they do not kill birds. For that reason I use them only. Rabbit gins are also responsible: in spite of the law, they are often set in the open: usually they kill or else

Opposite: Hen stonechat

G

maim birds beyond recovery. Rabbit wires also sometimes catch birds: I have released a partridge from one of them. Overhead wires are another source of danger: water-rails on autumn migration and also redwings and fieldfares have more than once been killed by them in or near Porlock. And then there is the motor car: the corpses on the highway testify to the peril it causes to small birds. The casual gunner is another frequent cause of mutilation. Surely everyone who calls himself a sportsman should have the decent humanity to recover a bird he has wounded.

How far, if at all, have birds any inherited memory of their prehistoric forebears? This question has often occurred to me when observing how buzzards, sparrow-hawks, kestrels and other hawks, after making a capture, spread their wings wide on the ground while holding their prey and plucking it. Is the mainspring of this action a dim, unconscious memory of the time when their primeval ancestors possessed and used the claws on their front limbs? The newly hatched hoatzin has them still, and they are present in the embryo of the domestic hen.

I will end this chapter by mentioning a bird problem which, though it concerns ornithologists and bird-lovers rather than birds, is now a very real one. Messrs. Ingram and Salmon in their book *Birds in Britain Today* protest against the 'intensive and American' methods of some modern ornithologists. They think that these 'highly specialised programmes' tend to convert what is really a sport or recreation into 'a ruthless business proposition'. This is very sane criticism. British ornithology is in danger of over-systematization: in some quarters there is no use for any bird observation that is not of what is called 'definite biological importance', a phrase capable of diverse interpretations. This attitude has its origin in a perfectly natural revulsion against the sugary sentimentality of the 'our feathered friends' type of writing. Both these extremes are to be avoided, but the work of the man whose approach to birds is primarily aesthetic is at least as valuable as the meticulous labours of the scientific card-index compiler. As Mr. W. K. Richmond says, in *Quest for Birds*, the true ornithologist must be one with an inner passion for birds. His scientific knowledge must supplement his pleasure in bird watching, but not destroy it. Galsworthy (in *Forsytes Pendyces and Others*) quoting Edward Garnett's dictum that 'we can never understand Nature unless we realise her emotionally,' wrote 'No man has ever realised Nature emotionally so completely as Hudson, and no writer has been so able to pass on to others that emotional realisation'. I need hardly add that I am not attempting to depreciate all modern scientific investigation into bird-life; much of it is of great value both to ornithologists and to amateur bird-lovers. What I do protest against is the arrogant assumption that no other approach to the study of birds is of any importance. I am glad to see that in the last volume of the new *Handbook of British Birds* the Editor writes that we are at the beginning of what it is not too much to call a new era in the study of birds in which the main emphasis is and will continue to be on the living bird and its problems.

CHAPTER XII

SOME BIRD BIOGRAPHIES

Besides the chaffinches mentioned in previous chapters, I have ringed with coloured rings a good many other birds which frequent our garden and the adjacent land.

The results, up to the end of 1942, though in some respects disappointing, reveal some facts worth recording. Greenfinches are temperamentally shy: I have never yet tamed one, and about half of those ringed never returned. Hen greenfinches are sometimes tame on the nest, and will sit almost till you touch them: but this betokens courage rather than confidence. Two remained with us for over a year, and two for over two years.

Two ringed blue tits were on feeding terms with us for about four and a half years. As they were both ringed early in the year they must then have been at least six or seven months old and so reached the respectable age of five years when they disappeared. One who stayed for nearly four years was an adult when ringed so he too lived nearly five years. Another was six years old when last seen, and one, ringed when an adult in February 1932, surprised us by reappearing in December 1941, and March 1942. This bird must have been over ten years old.

The marital affairs of one pair afforded some unusual incidents. In the early summer of 1939, No. 1, a cock, and No. 2, a hen, both ringed with coloured rings, mated and nested in a box to the north of our house. On May 4th the hen, No. 2, was sitting on seven eggs. No. 1, the cock, was constantly on a bird-table near another nesting box affixed to a crab-apple tree on the south of our house. Another tit, No. 3, unringed and presumably a female, was taking nesting material to this box. Yet another unringed blue tit, No. 4, presumably a cock, came twice to this box but was driven off once by No. 1 and once by No. 2.

During May 5th, No. 3 went on building in the 'crab' box. No. 1 was constantly on a bird-table nearby, and occasionally No. 2. There was frequent fighting between three tits, probably Nos. 1, 3, and 4, round the nesting box. No. 1 watched No. 3 building, but often followed and chased her when she was collecting nesting material. At the same time he was feeding his mate, No. 2, at the north nesting box. By nightfall the nest in the 'crab' box was partly built.

During May 6th the same state of affairs existed, but No. 3
seemed to do less building. A blue tit, probably No. 3, roosted in
that box that night and again on the night of May 7th. During that
day there was again constant fighting round the 'crab' box, but on
May 8th, though Nos. 1 and 2 occasionally visited the box, Nos. 3
and 4 were not seen and no further building took place. The nest,
which now contained one egg, was deserted.

The most probable interpretation of these facts seems to be that it
was a case of attempted bigamy by the cock, No. 1, with the hens
Nos. 2 and 3 and that this was resented by No. 4 (the other cock), and
eventually by No. 3 (the other hen), as she gave up building, and the
nest was deserted. The attitude of No. 2, the rightful mate of No. 1,
was more likely suspicious than complaisant. The fact that the cock,
No. 1, continued his marital attentions to her, while showing
interest in the other hen, is amusing or painful according to the
point of view. Nos. 1 and 2 mated again successfully in 1940.

A different pair of blue tits, both ringed with coloured rings for
identification, nested in a nesting box some twenty yards from our
windows in 1941. Eight eggs were laid, but the cock was unfortunately killed in a trap while the hen was still sitting; he had been
assiduous in feeding her. Seven young hatched out, and the hen, who
had lost her tail, as well as her mate, brought them up alone. When
only two days old they were fed on small green caterpillars. Two of
the fledglings flew on the sixteenth day after hatching; on the nine-
teenth day three only were left in the nesting box: two of these
emerged on the twenty-first day and the last one on the twenty-
second. The fledging period varies from fifteen to twenty-one days,
but is usually nineteen. Probably the stronger youngsters got more
than their fair share of the provender, for the last to fly was a
weakling. Had the other parent survived, the rationing might have
been better managed. When the young were about a week old,
I saw the hen making advances to another blue tit, which was
unringed. The stranger attempted coition with her, but if this was
an effort on the part of the hen to obtain a second mate to help her
bring up her family, it was unsuccessful, for she still fed them
alone. This gallant hen's success in rearing her large family unaided
deserves to be put on record.

Blackbirds seem to wander a good deal and I fear that many
become casualties in gardens when fruit is ripe. The persistence
with which they find their way through the nets which cover my
morello cherries is at times irritating even to a bird-lover: sparrow-
hawks also take their toll: I find blackbird kills in the garden, and

suspect that a hawk of this species—perhaps the one I caught and ringed in my fruit cage—is responsible. I have ringed over eighty blackbirds. Much of their private history is enshrined in my note-books, but little of it is of general interest. However, the musical career of a cock is worthy of more particular notice. He had a most lovely voice and sometimes fluted just outside my bedroom window of a morning.

In the spring and summer of 1936 he sang from various stances near the house, and introduced two musical phrases into his chanson; the one first heard in March was simple:—

a three-note phrase which he constantly interpolated among a normal blackbird melody. But by mid-May this had been elaborated into a longer *motif*, thus:—

Evidently this cheerful theme pleased him; for he yodelled it over and over again. It was last heard on July 6th, a late date. His mate nested in a bundle of pea-sticks and as I saw him brooding the eggs he was evidently an exemplary and hard-working spouse.

Throughout the spring and summer of 1937 and 1938 he sang lustily, but without introducing any fresh musical theme, and shared the duties of bringing up several families. He became remarkably tame, and would run right up to my feet for pine-kernels. In the spring of 1939 his song showed a surprising musical development. My wife, in a letter to *Country Life*, described it thus:—

'I have been greatly interested this spring in the development by three distinct stages of a musical phrase in the song of a blackbird.

. . . Early this year I noticed him constantly using among his avian whistlings and chucklings the first phrase indicated, and remarked to my husband, "Our blackbird is singing 'The Death of Nelson'!" ("England expects.") Later on he produced the last line of a Moody and Sankey hymn ("A day's march nearer home") by adding a note at the beginning and slightly altering the rhythm, (the second figure). Finally, the song developed even more ambitiously into the third phrase, and apparently he takes much pride and pleasure in it, shouting it with great gusto—normally in the key of F♯ or C♯—from roof or tree, bird-table or ground. It became, in fact, his signature tune and is included at least once in every recital.'

In 1940 his song deteriorated, and some time in June he disappeared. He was at least six years old, a good age for a blackbird, though one is recorded as having reached nine years.

Another blackbird I have been able to identify not only from his ring but by a white shoulder spot, which has survived or is renewed annually after his autumn moult ever since I first made his acquaintance in 1935, so that he also is now (1942) seven years old.

Here I may mention that not only cock but hen blackbirds fight furiously in springtime. It is difficult to say how far these combats are territorial, but if they are, then it looks as if the hens assisted in staking out and defending the breeding area. Or these battles may be simply feminine jealousy.

The ways of dunnocks (or hedge sparrows) are difficult to fathom: they appear to be a furtive and nomadic race. It has more than once happened that when I think I have ringed all our local dunnocks, a new unmarked one has appeared out of the blue, and many of them fade out unaccountably, which suggests a high mortality rate. I have ringed sixty. Three of these lived for nearly three years. There is another, a hen, whose life history contains some incidents worth relating. As I ringed her in March 1937, her career must have begun not later than the spring or summer of 1936. I saw her taking food to her young during the early summer of 1937, but at the end of June she disappeared and did not return till mid-November, soon after the first frost. During the early part of 1938 she consorted with at least three separate dunnocks, but although she came to our bird-tables throughout that summer I did not ascertain with whom she mated, nor could I find her nest. In mid-July she vanished for the second time, and was not seen till the end of December, again after hard frost. During the severe weather of early 1939 she constantly patronised our bird-tables, and in March mated with a ringed cock. Without assistance from her mate, she built a nest in one of our macrocarpa hedges and three young, fed by both parents, were successfully reared. For the rest of that year both she and her spouse paid us rather irregular visits, but in March and April 1940 the same couple mated again and I saw them taking food to their young.

The hen once more disappeared from August to October; after that the pair were in evidence till January, and the hen till April, 1941. Then she suddenly performed another vanishing trick, which lasted for a whole year, for I did not see her again till April 1942, when I found her building a nest in a creeper behind our garage. The three young were fed by her and a new mate, also ringed. Her companion of 1939 and 1940 lost the tip of his upper mandible, probably in one of those snap mouse-traps which maim so many birds; we did not see him after May 1941; probably he perished of semi-starvation. The hen is still with us and must now be nearly seven years old. I have several times seen her singing, as female robins sometimes do. The fact that she mated with the same cock for two successive years suggests that, barring accidents, dunnocks, too, pair for life. Her shorter absences were probably attributable to a plentiful supply elsewhere. Her disappearance for a whole year may be due to her having found a mate who had acquired rights over another territory.

Song thrushes are here scarcer than blackbirds: they do not seem so hardy a race and probably suffer more in severe weather. I have ringed nearly forty. One of these was brought to me by a neighbour's gardener in January 1941; it was in a very enfeebled condition, the result of over a month's persistent east winds, with snow and frost. I endeavoured to resuscitate the patient with warmth and whisky, but it survived only an hour. This bird was over four and a half years old. Another was four years old when last seen.

A ringed thrush was an unwilling actor in a rather curious incident. He had captured and was about to dispose of a worm just outside my study window when a kestrel swooped down from over the house, snatched his prey from him, devoured it and perched for a few seconds on the bird-table before flying away. I knew that kestrels ate earth-worms occasionally but had never before caught one at it.

A fledgling song-thrush ringed in July 1933 was not seen until May 1934, when she returned and built a perfectly normal nest in our macrocarpa hedge from which the young flew in June. This shows that song thrushes sometimes breed when under a year old.

My ringing experiments have shown me how impossible it is to identify robins or indeed any bird by behaviour alone: to rely on this at once leads to error. But there was, before my ringing days, a redbreast whose confiding habits made him readily identifiable, even before I marked him, as described below.

It was in the autumn that we first made his acquaintance, or rather he forced his acquaintance upon us, for he appeared from nowhere in particular while we were tidying up the garden for the winter. An offer of sultanas, always acceptable to robins, appealed to him at once: (we had not then discovered pine-kernels). Soon he was taking them from our hands, and in a week or two he would come for them from quite a distance when he heard a whistle. He would perch confidingly on my wife's shoulder, hop down her arm to her hand and stand there during his repast. He even faced the photographer in this pose with complete nonchalance. We called him 'Christopher Robin', or 'Christopher' for short.

He had his moods. He would perch upon a post or pea-stick, put his head on one side and look at you expectantly. You would, in obedience to this dumb demand, produce from a tin box in your waistcoat pocket a selection of perfectly sound sultanas, and proffer them in your outstretched fingers. He would simply stand and stare, deaf to all allurements; having thus made you feel a fool, he would as like as not turn his back on you, and then dive into a herbaceous border. Other habits were entirely charming: to see him, when athirst, delicately sip a dew-drop from a blade of grass, was to admire a graceful act perfectly performed. Occasionally he visited us indoors, but always preserved complete composure, entering and departing by the same window, and not fluttering stupidly against the glass.

With the New Year we noticed a change in his behaviour. Sometimes he was absent all day. Now and again he sang softly, a low, liquid warble which rippled his red throat. Early in February he appeared in company with another robin, a very shy one who always fled when I approached. Sometimes the newcomer chased Christopher. We began to have doubts as to 'his' sex, for hitherto he had driven off all red-breasted intruders.

Wishing to be able to follow his career with certainty, I tried to drop a spot of green paint upon him as an identification mark, when he was feeding from my hand, but he suddenly flew against the paint brush and so tipped one of his wings with green, and marked himself.

During the next six or seven weeks his behaviour was puzzling. In cold weather he was as tame as ever, but when the climate was milder he disappeared. On several occasions he was involved in conversations with other robins which appeared to be definitely of a matrimonial nature.

Then, in the third week of March, my wife saw our green-tipped robin with a beakful of moss: 'he' was busy nest-building! After this 'Christopher' became 'Christina': her behaviour was so obviously feminine. She abandoned the first nest when completed, built another and laid five eggs, but still at times came off the nest to feed from our hands. This nest, which was not on our land, was robbed, but a third effort was entirely successful, and she hatched off her young safely. But at the end of June Christina departed and never came back.

A cock robin which I ringed with coloured rings in January 1942 subsequently became involved in matrimonial or semi-matrimonial tangles which are both curious and interesting. As his adventures concern five robins, four of them ringed with coloured rings and the fifth unringed, it is best, in order to keep their identities separate, to distinguish them by the numbers which they bear in my schedules of ringed birds.

On April 27th a cock, 52, was feeding a hen, 54, on my bird-table, and again on May 3rd. Another hen, 57, in March and April built a nest in the bank of a hedge in my garden, and was, during this period, constantly accompanied by an unringed cock. She hatched out the first week in May, and on the 5th I was amazed to find cock 52 assisting her to feed her young. The unringed cock, her first mate, had disappeared, and I never saw him again. The two robins, 52 and 57, continued to feed these young, which left the nest on May 18th.

The hen robin, 54 (52's original mate), I believe built a nest in the lane near my house, but I could not find it; it was probably destroyed or deserted, for I never saw any food carried in its direction. On May 23rd and 25th the cock, 52, was again in company with his first mate, 54, and was feeding her; on the 26th in the morning he was again on the bird-table with 54 and in the evening with 57, but he paid no attention to either of them. Finally on June 13th he appeared several times on the table with a fresh robin, 53, which I had not seen since February. As there was no fighting between them I conclude that 53 was yet another hen, for two males would certainly have fought: she was taking food away from the bird-table.

The hen, 57, disappeared at the end of May, and the hen, 54, early in June. Hen, 53, was present till July 8th and the cock, 52, till the 16th, but then all four vanished—a way that robins have after the mating season. Having regard to the disappearance of the original mate of the hen, 57, it would be unfair to accuse the cock, 52, of bigamy, especially as his original mate, 54, seems to have failed to rear a family. Rather, his assisting the widow to feed her young may be regarded as chivalrous. But his relations with three separate females, more or less contemporaneously, appear to have been at least questionable.

Since 1932 I have ringed over sixty robins. Four of these lived for over two years. (Mr. Burkitt, the well-known authority on robins, estimates their average life at from 2·8 to one and one-eighth years.) The rest, though they would provide material for a monograph, are not of general interest. Many which were present with us all through the winter disappeared from our ken early in the year, probably to find and fight for suitable breeding territories. Some of them returned in the autumn, but most of them vanished completely.

One robin was tame enough to come into my study and demand to be fed. To hear the friction of her claws as she alighted on a chair back, and see her perched there asking for a kernel, always gave me a thrill. But someone wooed her away from me. I came across her once in an ivied tree in a neighbour's land but there she was not of a coming on disposition. She stayed only two months.

One pair, after mating and nesting together in 1938, resumed companionship in the spring of 1939. Presumably they would have shared a brood together that year, but, perhaps owing to some catastrophe, the cock disappeared in April.

The way in which so many of my ringed robins have faded away is disconcerting. For instance, in the spring of 1937 there were five unringed robins about our garden, and no ringed ones, though since September 1935 I had ringed twelve. What happens to the absentees? I have mentioned above Mr. Burkitt's calculations which show that their average lives are short, and I know from experience that the mortality among young robins is heavy. But they do not all die young. There are records of redbreasts eight and eleven years old. The fact that they bathe at dusk in winter with the thermometer as low as 25° Fahr. shows that they are hardy.

There is a considerable migration of British robins from north to south in autumn, and birds ringed in England have travelled as far as sixty miles from the place of ringing by the spring and early summer of the following year. Some robins ringed in England have been recovered on the continent. And Mr. W. R. Philipson has recorded in British Birds (Vol. XXXIII, p. 247) a robin seen at sea, 28th September 1939, midway between Cape Clear and the Azores, i.e. about 500 miles south-west of Ireland and very nearly as far west of Spain. There is also migration of the continental robin to our shores.

I have myself seen migrating robins on the Porlock seaboard in November.

The theory has recently been advanced that posturing of robins—head strained back and breast displayed—is used exclusively in territorial defence and is not employed in courtship. With this view I definitely disagree, and so do the cock robins who posture to hens in my garden. They do not seem to have heard of the theory. Perhaps the use of posturing in courtship is gradually lapsing, but it has not yet ceased. It is well known that the same physical action is often employed by birds to express different emotions.[1]

To some this chapter may seem to be much ado about nothing. But some facts of importance have emerged—the constancy of a pair of chaffinches during the bringing up of three families, the survival of individual blue tits for five, six and ten years, the mating of one pair of them for two successive seasons, the breeding of a young song-thrush in its first year, the evolution of a blackbird's song, and the seven years' story of a dunnock's life. Ringing has also shown, as I suspected, that our garden population is by no means constant and also that the lives of most of our smaller *passeres* do not usually exceed two or three years.

I think that these endeavours to trace the individual histories of wild birds are at least as intelligent and interesting as the census making and card indexing which seems with some modern ornithologists to be becoming an obsession. I have got to know many of my ringed birds intimately: they have become friends and companions, and ceased to be merely casual acquaintances or specimens. And another mild excitement is the return of a ringed bird after an absence sometimes of several months. To me, at any rate, my experiments have given pleasure and insight into creatures different in character but 'nearer to earth', in the Meredithean sense, than we are. To walk round the garden and see half a dozen or more wild birds fly towards you, and either feed from your hand or pick up kernels or sultanas at your feet is to me—and to others—a delightful experience.

[1] The subject is discussed in Mr. D. Lack's book *The Life of the Robin*, published after my MS. was in the printers' hands.—E. W. H.

CHAPTER XIII

BIRDS AND LANDSCAPES

Mr. W. B. Richmond in *England's Birds*, writing of the Northumbrian fells, says that the presence of certain species of birds 'here changes the bleakness into wildness, converts a forbidding scene of desolation into a haunting, mysterious wilderness'. And Dr. Vaughan-Cornish in the *Poetic Impression of Natural Scenery* relates how in the Rother Valley he found that the river no longer gave him complete satisfaction, until a dipper came into view, bowing, diving and swimming. This changed everything: 'the river, the banks, the meadow and the trees all grouped themselves about the stone where stood the dainty, white-throated bird.'

All real bird-lovers must recall similar sensations. A cock blackbird, prospecting for the unwary worm on a square of lawn, windsheltered on two sides by cypress hedges, at once completes the picture: the lawn ceases to be a mere plot of grass and becomes a precinct wherein he may serenely take his pleasure. Similarly the kingfisher, flying so low over the river that he seems to glide upon its limpid surface, a jewel of cobalt and green, or hovering, an azure scintillation, above a shallow, brings the spirit of the tropic forests to a Devon trout-stream. How often has a bird supplied the one thing needed to perfect an Exmoor landscape. The sudden croak of a raven, unseen till heard, recreates in an instant the primeval, untameable character of Exmoor moorland.

The tower of Luccombe Church near Porlock is one of the most beautiful in Somerset; its slender simplicity of structure is enhanced by the cypresses which grow beside it, and the mellow texture of its stone blends with its environment. Seen from the steep lane leading from the village towards Wootton Courtenay, the tower is framed on either hand by tall hedges: the row of dark cypresses slopes up to it from left to right, where the tallest of them creeps up an angle of the tower; then there comes a gap through which gleams the tower itself, and thence the cypresses descend gradually to the right. The contrast between the swart colours of the cypress rank and the tower's lighter tones adds charm to the picture. One evening in December, as the sunset afterglow shone upon its western face, a kestrel suddenly swooped down and disappeared uncannily into the mouth of a grotesque gargoyle which leans out from near the summit.

That a bird which winnows the most turbulent winds with its pinions should find here its haven for the hours of darkness set a seal of peace upon the scene.

In the copse opposite our gate are two white poplars whose leaves glisten against a background of green elms and blue sky. In the morning light, when a wind flutters them, their upturned fronds flicker like the whites of eyes; but when gulls fly above them they turn to flecks of foam upon a restless sea.

Weir Water and Chalk Water are two typical Exmoor coombes. Both flow from south to north into Oare Water, which, after meeting Badgworthy Water lower down, joins the River Lyn above Lynmouth. Each has its own peculiar beauty. Weir Water is the wilder, for its sides are more precipitous and its stream hurries more tumultuously. The contorted oaks in Weir Wood have an elf-like charm, and the ruins of the farmstead which in part it encloses, create that aura of sadness which clings to deserted human habitations. Chalk Water is broader and more open: there is not that shut-in sensation—perhaps an atavistic relic—which sometimes oppresses. Both coombes divide into triple or quadruple arms towards their sources. Deep little goyals have fiercely carved their way into the sides of both waters; solitary rowans or stunted oaks adorn them: there is an intimate secrecy about their recesses. Fancifully, the two coombes are like two beautiful women: one wild and dark, the other fair and tranquil.

Bird life in both these coombes is prolific, especially in summer. But the ring ousel is for me the typical bird of Weir Water. Its song is wilder than the mistle thrush's but not so sweet as the blackbird's. It speaks the very spirit of the moors. Weir Water, even in April can be bleak and desolate, but the ring ousel's song makes it more homely; the sight of him perched on stone wall or stunted thorn, pouring out his careless, defiant carol, gives a finishing touch to a moorland landscape.

Chalk Water also possesses a varied wild life, both animal and avian. I have watched a long, lithe, tawny vixen, with darker brush, white-tipped, run sinuously along the coombe side, slither down to the stream and cross fastidiously by stepping stones to vanish among a forest of green fern. Deer, especially when silhouetted on the skyline, are always the crowning glory of Exmoor scenery. Another day in Chalk Water a group of stags stood at gaze upon a heathery shoulder, and, thus posed, made the picture perfect. But of birds it is a buzzard, soaring higher and higher in ever-widening circles, that completes the ideal setting for this Water. As you gaze upwards at the great bird's indolent flight you realize the marvellous perspective of a 'bird's eye' view, and see in imagination the whole valley spread out beneath you.

There are bays on the West Somerset sea-board which at low tide present a grey and dreary waste of sand, mud and water. But let a curlew wing its way across the sea's dim margin, calling wistfully, and at once the whole scene loses its melancholy.

One May morning as I stood under one of our cherry-trees, flooded with dead-white blossoms, there was a chime of silver bird-notes, and two goldfinches flitted down to settle amid its branches. As a spray swayed beneath their feather-weight their crimson and gold flashed in sunlight against a background of dazzling whiteness. Here was a memory to keep and a vignette ready and posed for an artist's palette.

Rey Coombe, just above Horner Green, at 8 o'clock on a July morning is as quiet a spot as you could desire. Since May the scene has entirely changed: the freshness of spring is merged in the maturity of summer. The foliage of oak and birch is dulled; even at that early hour the leaves seem weary and relaxed beneath the sun's scorching. Ashes, the last to break into leaf, no longer wear their bright livery. Growing bracken has smoothed the roughness of coombe-sides with a filmy mantle of green. Amidst the fern, fox-gloves' splendour is waning as their bells fall silently, one by one. The scent of honeysuckle, wreathing dead alders, is languorous, and lies heavy on the air. There is no wind except wayward gusts fluttering the ashes' leaf-fringes. Of bird-song there is little—the half-hearted notes of a distant thrush, the cool liquid calls of nut-hatches, and the disjointed warble of a blackcap; but still wood-pigeons coo to each other in cosseting tones; they are always making love. Suddenly a cock redstart shoots out into the sunlight: as he hovers a moment, his fire-tail, a ruby jewel in a setting of jade, adds the flash of colour that was wanting to perfect the picture.

Another day in mid-May presented a very different scene. A bitterly cold wind from the north brought rain which, in the afternoon, for two hours, turned to snow. Never before had I seen it lie upon blossoms of wistaria and laburnum.[1] Dunkery and its sister hills, snow-covered, were plunged in this short space from summer into winter. Two jet-black carrion crows, crying hoarsely above a blanched landscape, completed the scene of desolation.

Sometimes snow comes stealthily, like the sound of muffled footsteps following in your wake; or it may be driven like spindrift

[1] 17th May, 1935

before a north-easter to lie in three-foot drifts beneath hedge-banks. One February dawn revealed the road over Dunkery a white ribbon across heathery moorland sparsely snow-covered. The moon hung in her last quarter above Crawter; the sky was clear and windless: thus clothed in white the hills draw nearer to you. On such a day I have found bullfinches, twelve hundred feet up, feeding upon the seeds of ling which the snowfall had not flattened. The sight of these little birds, happy in seemingly inhospitable surroundings, the rich russets of their breasts—the colour of old bricks in sunlight—glowing like live coals, banished at once all the cheerlessness from a scene which but for them embodied the harsh rigours of moorland winter.

One morning in March a grey transparency veiled the sides of Hawkcombe, and in its sheltered recesses there was a calm, so still that hardly a quiver stirred the needles of brindled larches; through sparse hedge-rows on the skyline opalescent light gleamed fitfully. A gentle tranquillity brooded over the wooded valley, broken only by the booming of foghorns from blinded ships in the distant Channel. Colours were all subdued into a harmony of pale browns and greys in tune with the tense silence. The calm was suddenly broken by the screeches of a rabble of jays, rising from a feast of acorns below the twisted, stunted oaks. With crests erect, like hair on end, they screamed from contorted thorns, and then with sinister suddenness vanished into the woodland. Dame Juliana Berners wrote of 'an unkindness of ravens'; she might have added to her list 'a profanity of jays', for, indeed their mouths are ever full of curses. Their raucous cries shattered the peaceful silence and turned the quiet coombe into a hag-ridden Gehenna.

Heather, both ling and the two heaths, cross-leaved and fine-leaved, floods the moor in August. The waxen flowers of the cross-leaved, faintly flushed with rose, have a delicacy which surpasses the deeper crimson or purple of the fine-leaved and of the ling, and their beauty is enhanced when they grow, as they sometimes do, in masses amid the yellow-green of partly unfurled fern. Dunkery glows deep purple in the light of a declining sun, with the deeper shadows nestling in its coombes, in honey-scented air. A cock stonechat, prinked out with russet breast, black cap and snowy collar, tossing himself upwards from a spray of gorse and then falling from heaven to another perch, completes a typical moorland landscape.

The blackbird's song, heard at dawn on an April morning, makes me sure that spring really has come. Perched on the low roof of the

Opposite; (*above*) Greenshank in act of sitting down on her nest
(*below*) Spotted flycatcher on nest

log-shed, he overflows into a fluting strain so penetrating that he seems to be singing in my bedroom instead of outside the open windows. His voice wanders, a thin, gold thread, among my dreams, cool as brooks rippling over mossy boulders; it brings back the faint, delicate scent of primroses in dewy orchards, the shy grace of violets—all the gracious sounds and sights and smells of spring.

Another April day, in a lonely coombe near Hurlstone Point, a solitary blackbird, perched on the topmost spray of a briary tangle, was warbling desultory snatches on bird Pan-pipes: after a shower his sleek, sable feathers and orange-tawny bill glistened wet in the sunshine: the dripping bracken glowed like old copper: the rain-sprinkled screes were mauve and lavender, flecked with faint red. Why had he chosen this barren, windswept goyal for his abode, when there are sheltered copses in the valley? Perhaps for him this is home, and for that he loves it, a poor thing but his own. And his presence there composed a featureless landscape into a picture.

There are two parallel rows, each of half-a-dozen ornamental crabs and cherries, which we call 'the avenue', leading from the end of our lawn to the gate into the 'untidy garden'. The dry summer of 1933 must have had some hidden virtue which urged their blossoming to exuberance in the spring of 1934. *Pyrus malus atrapurpurea*, for so the nurseryman's catalogue will have it, was so crammed with crimson flower that its coppery leaves were scarcely visible. At ten years old, it was ten feet high, and its branches sprawled out to the same width. Next to it stands *cerasus serratifolia*, a cherry with dead-white double blossoms, hanging in bell-clusters: a glimpse of these snowy blooms against the massed crimson of the *pyrus*, with deep blue sky beyond, made you hold your breath. Further down the row is a *pyrus malus floribunda*, and indeed that year it lived up to its name, for its pale green foliage was overwhelmed by a foam of delicate, rose-blushed blossom, flowing along every branch from its tip to the tree's trunk. Looking along this row, pale pink, snow-white and deep crimson were backed by the goldy-green of sprouting corn, and beyond that purple moor rising to azure heaven.

Loveliness, indeed: but a woodlark, heard at first distantly, then nearer and overhead, leaping with half-closed wings into the wind as he rose in irregular ellipses, and spilling sweet, desultory drops of song like the 'gentle rain from heaven', now unconscious mimicry of philomela, now his own pearls of melody, brought perfection to a spring morning. Thus Euterpe's lyric flute crowned the joy of Flora's revels.

Waking one October morning, while it was scarcely light I

Opposite: Woodlark at nest

looked out upon an Exmoor landscape which belied Keats' 'Season of mists and mellow fruitfulness'. The mellowness, the rich fecundity was there, but though the sky was not entirely cloudless, the atmosphere was singularly clear and luminous. No wind stirred. The fields, a patchwork of yellows, greens and reds, lay quiet as though resting after the labours of summer fertility; the elms stood listening —perhaps thinking—in silence. Though autumn sometimes suggests evanescence and decay, this morning the world was new-born; 'half-strange seemed Earth, and sweeter than her flowers.' Everything was waiting, breathless, in expectancy as for the unfolding of some impending mystery. Each dawn brings forth a new day, but only rarely does its birth suggest that the miracle of creation is being re-enacted in our very sight.

Every sunrise is a revelation, though we sleepy-heads often miss its wonder and delight. Soon the eastern sky glowed like a skein of silk, shot with rose and orange, and then, as the orb emerged, flared an angry red, fading to gold, and later to pure blue freaked with silvery white cloud. Across this sky came rooks and jackdaws cawing and chattering in cheery conversation, dropping in corkscrew dives to the stubble fields, rich with spilled grain. They broke the spell, but turned the view, framed by my bedroom window, into a landscape picture.

From the same window we look out over pasture and ploughland to where, emerging from a belt of firs, the Dunkery Hill Gate Road strikes bravely in a curving course along the naked slope of Robin Howe, a bosomed hill, with two barrows for nipples, which forms the eastermost bastion of the Dunkery range. We used to call it 'the Red Road' because its surface was that lovely shade of deep red which comes from the crumbling of sandstone. Winding upwards aslant the moor, it leads the eye to the skyline. Even after your eye has traced its graceful windings to the top of the ridge, your mind follows its meanderings till it joins the old road from Dunster to Dulverton. Somewhere it must have crossed Blackmore's 'Doone Path'. It is thirty-five years and more since first I came down the road at the end of a day's bicycle ride along the Brendons. Little did I think then that I should ever live where every morning I look out upon it from my bedroom window.

It is the road which gives character to the landscape; it divides two stretches of moorland, and thus groups them. We know the road in all seasons and in all conditions. It has become our friend. When the mist has cleared, or after a shower, its surface has shone deep red beneath a rainbow's iris; scorched in hot sunshine it has gleamed a pale rose. Drifting snow, piled against its banks, transforms it into a white scarf dropped carelessly across swart moorland. But it is when a pair of ravens fly over it, croaking eerily, that the landscape receives its finishing touch: they complete Nature's unconscious handiwork.

(This *was* our Red Road. But now the County Council in their wisdom have coated it with tar-mac. Our Red Road has become a black snake that wriggles and squirms its sable coil malevolently upwards. The Red Road stood for quiet and peace; it belonged to the unhurried past; this black reptile portends speed; it belongs to the present with its feverish quest of the unessential.)

Butterflies, with their bright and varied colours can, in the same way as birds, add the essential note of beauty to some familiar scene. There is a lavender hedge alongside of one of our garden paths, haunted by innumerable bees, both honey and humble, whose humming mingles with its aromatic scent. The grey-green of its fronds is as lovely as an afterglow viewed through veils of mist. But a Red Admiral, in scarlet, black and white, is the gem needed for this setting. And similarly, a Peacock butterfly, settling on a snowy sheet of blackthorn to fan its iridescent wings, raises loveliness to the peak of perfection.

Words are like birds: they have wings, and songs and plumage of many bright and tender hues which glow and sparkle and wane. But though we turn them this way and that, like gems, to show the light lurking in each facet, we know that they can never express all the beauty of which we are conscious, and still less that which the senses touch but rarely, in moments of mysterious exaltation.

Robert Bridges, in *The Testament of Beauty* says:

> *Man's happiness, his flaunting honey'd flower of soul,*
> *Is his loving response to the wealth of Nature.*

He responds to colour, in sky, flower, sea and earth. And the sight of the bird which belongs to the particular scene heightens and completes that happiness.

GOLDFINCHES AND CHERRY BLOSSOM

> *Wind-ruffled in misty moonlight,*
> *The white flowers of our cherries*
> *Against swart masses of cypress*
> *Flutter like myriad ermine moths,*
> *Or like wan ghosts of melodies half-forgotten,*
> *Or woodland dryads, virginal, ethereal.*

At noon their cool petals glisten in sunlight,
And goldfinches, pranked and pied in crimson black and gold,
Glitter and flicker amid their florets,
Dropping notes silver and golden,
Lightly weighing down the blossom-laden branches,
Creating joy, wonder and thankfulness
For that while all around us are death and destruction
Beauty of bird and flower endure,
Immutable, indestructible.

CHAPTER XIV

THE QUANTOCKS

You might call the Quantocks 'Exmoor in Miniature', for indeed they reproduce that country on a smaller scale. The highest point rises at Wills Neck only to 1261 feet, and few of their summits exceed eleven hundred: their coombes are less lengthy: the scenery is milder, just as the Exmoor landscape is less rugged and uncouth than Dartmoor with its stark tors. But it is a homely, friendly land, essentially English in its peaceful beauty, and most of it is in August and September blessedly less frequented by the more turbulent type of tripper than Exmoor's over-advertised 'beauty spots'.

Seen from the Minehead-Taunton or Minehead-Bridgewater roads, which run roughly south and north of the range, the Quantock Hills look like one unbroken, whale-humped mass, scarred at intervals by coombes and topped in places by beech hedges; you would expect on reaching their summit to be able at once to look down on the other side. But you would be deceived. Unsuspected valleys lie between, branches of the larger coombes that run up from the lower-lying country on either side.

The principal valleys on the northern side are Holford and Hodder's Coombes, divided by a hill called Hare Knap. These, as they ascend, spread out into three or four goyals, clothed with gracious oaks that recall Horner and Nutscale Waters. Any of them lead you, faint yet pursuing, over stony tracks, to sweeps of ling that stretch in an infinite variety of lilac, purple and lavender, spangled with the gold of dwarf gorse, and the russet and green of whortleberry: a carpet whose pattern is daedalian. Never, even on my own Exmoor, have I seen ling in more luxuriant beauty than in September on the Quantocks. In sunlight its iridescence, mingled with the gorse's sheen, almost dazzles your sight. In spring some of the coombes are starred with wood anemones—windflowers. Their presence is grateful to me, for they do not grace our Exmoor coombes.

Beech grows well on the Quantocks: there are some fine, tall trees in Crowcombe Park, and along the old coach road which climbs the ridge above Alfoxton Park there are some gigantic beeches: though some are in decay there is one very beautiful row still standing whose contours recall Corot's pictures. Beech hedges enclose either side of the prehistoric track which traverses the summits of the Quantocks from Will's Neck to Beacon Hill above Bicknoller. Some knolls are crowned by groups of Scots pines, and in Alfoxton Park there is a venerable oak whose history must reach back at any rate to mediaeval times. In Wind Down Clump at the northern end of the Quantocks there is a tall, battered fir which stands out conspicuously from all the surrounding country.

The Quantocks are seamed with winding lanes in which it is quite easy to get lost. But they are full of delightful surprises. One day a fox stepped daintily across the path a few paces in front of me, stopped to investigate some subtle scent, and vanished with a spring into woody undergrowth. You will find little lost hamlets and farms, often thatched, and festooned with purple clematis, entirely aloof and sequestered from this age of hurry and turmoil. Time here stands still: it is so quiet that you can almost hear the trees breathing.

Bicknoller Coombe, which leads you up from Bicknoller Village to Bicknoller Post, is a typical Quantock coombe. It winds upwards between steep banks, clothed purple and gold in gorse and heather: the stream which tumbles and rushes down by the side of the track sings sweet old folk-tunes to you as you walk or rest to take your breath. Stonechats and whinchats pop up suddenly to the tops of bramble-bushes 'chacking' and 'ticking' at you. Aloft a kestrel hangs suspended against fathomless blue.

The Quantocks stand back from Exmoor and its satellite uplands to the west and south, and tower above the lowlands of the Parrett Vale to the north and east. So placed their highest ridges present a bird's (or rather 'hawk's') eye view of some of the loveliest country in south-west England. I know no finer prospect than that which looks northwards from the hills above Alfoxton Park. Its variety is its especial charm, for its contrasts are innumerable. Over gently descending slopes you look across Bridgewater Bay and the Severn Sea, with its twin islands Flat and Steep Holm, to the Welsh coast and misty mountains; in and out of the low and level flats the Parrett river winds sinuously, and beyond, Brean Down and Brent Knoll rise abruptly from the plain. The Polden Hills form but a gentle excrescence in the middle distance; on their further side Glastonbury Tor still watches over the Isle of Avalon. The long, low line of the Mendips fades into sky and cloud on the horizon. The colours of this unbelievable landscape vary every hour, almost every minute, from green to grey and silver and purple with the vicissitudes of light and shade; sometimes the whole scene dreams in a gentle haze.

From Cothelstone Beacon the panorama is as wide and broad, but from here it stretches over the Vale of Taunton Deane to the Blackdown and Brendon Hills, and further to the Haldon ridge beyond Exeter, and the faint silhouettes of Dartmoor's bastions and sentinel tors. Exmoor, topped by Dunkery Beacon, stands out clear-cut in the middle distance. Turn your eyes north-eastwards and you can follow the silver-scimitar line of the Parrett meandering seawards, backed by the mounded mass of the Mendips. East and south-east are spread all the gentle uplands of Dorset and further still the remote grey downs skirting Salisbury Plain. It is good on a warm windless day in late summer to lie here on the springy turf and absorb the blessed peacefulness of the scene.

There are red-deer on the Quantocks, though not so many as on Exmoor, Foxes are plentiful. Except for an occasional peregrine and buzzard, the larger hawks seem less common than they are on Exmoor. Ravens you may see now and then. Green woodpeckers are abundant even up to the 1000 feet line, and there are a number of blackcock. Grey wagtails and dippers haunt the streams: one 'water colley' had made her nest between the wall of a weir and the water flowing over it.

Alfoxton Park, near Holford, is celebrated from its association with William and Dorothy Wordsworth, who lived there for a year in 1797-8. Wordsworthians will remember Dorothy's description of the view from the exquisitely proportioned Georgian house which was until the war a very comfortable private hotel. Though the house has been enlarged, and altered, that view has not much changed since she wrote; the high hill to the south is no longer topped with fern, for trees have been planted along its summit, but the wood whose round top 'has the appearance of a mighty dome', with its undergrowth of hollies, is still there, and so also are the deer. There is no longer a view of the sea from Dorothy's sitting room for that window has been blocked. The 'glen at the bottom of the wood' is much overgrown, but it is possible to identify the waterfall which the poet and his sister loved so much.

It was at Alfoxton that the Wordsworths' friendship with Samuel Taylor Coleridge ripened, and thence they went together on the famous walk to Watchet and Lynton, during which the *Rime of the Ancient Mariner* was conceived. The asses, which a hundred years ago pastured under the hollies, were partly responsible for *Peter Bell*, and it was a hail shower from which he sheltered under these same trees that Wordsworth described in *A whirl-blast from behind the hill*. In *Tintern Abbey*, though the famous lines were not composed till just after the Wordsworths had left Alfoxton, there is evidently much that was inspired by memories of the Quantocks:—

> let the moon
> Shine on thee in thy solitary walk;
> And let the misty mountain winds be free
> To blow against thee.

The shore of the Bristol Channel at Lilstock and at Kilve, a mile or two north of the Quantocks, is forbidding, and sinister; the low crumbling cliffs are formed of contorted strata whose sombre tints shade from pale grey to indigo; at low tide pools of slimy water lie between flat slabs of slaty rock along the shore, over which disconsolate herons brood despondently. But at sunset shafts of slanting light gild a pathway thence over Minehead Bay to the North Hill and the outlying bastions of Exmoor. In its radiance the eerie gloom of this hard-featured shore is for the moment dispelled.

The migration along the coastline here, and also at East Quantoxhead, is interesting in spring and autumn. I have found flocks of pied wagtails, numbering sometimes fifty or more, resting on the cliffs near Kilve in August and September. There is in spring, and probably also in autumn, a migration of swallows and house and sandmartins in contrary directions, both eastwards and westwards, along the shore, and the same holds good as regards swallows through the Quantocks further inland. In fact the 'double' migration which I notice every year at Porlock evidently continues further east in this district of West Somerset.

At Stolford, further to the east, the coast is to me less forbidding: a shingle ridge keeps back the sea and Bridgewater Bay sweeps in a gracious curve towards the Burnham sandhills. Inland lie level stretches of rough grass-land. In early autumn the shore and bay are frequented by turnstones, whimbrel, sheld-duck and redshank: goldfinches, in flocks of thirty or forty, haunt thistle-clumps at the shingle's edge and among them are wheatears and gaudy yellow wagtails, all on their return journey.

CHAPTER XV

BLACKCOCK AND BLUEBELLS ON EXMOOR

Black grouse have flourished on Exmoor from time immemorial, while red grouse, though they have been introduced on several occasions, and still persist in small numbers, do not seem to flourish, perhaps because the climate is not suitable: they prefer higher altitudes, and Dunkery Beacon, our highest hill, is only 1708 feet. Even black game are certainly not now as common on Exmoor as they were some thirty years ago; blackcock we see in fair numbers, but grey hens are scarce. I have been told that this is due to the fact that too many grey hens have been shot, sometimes under the mistaken impression that they were red grouse.

Heath poults, to use the local name for black grouse, are wary birds and near approach to them is usually difficult. But when the blackcock are engaged in their nuptial display it is easy to obtain a good view of this curious performance by means of a motor-car, provided that the 'lekking' place is so situated that a car can be driven near to it. There is one spot on western Exmoor where this can be done, at the top of Hawkcombe on the Porlock-Exford road, where the Devon and Somerset Stag-hounds meet. Here is a smooth stretch of grass surrounded on three sides by thick heather, and on the other by the road; a car can be driven on to the grass, except in very wet weather, but even from the road birds can be watched quite well at a distance of only twenty or thirty yards.

The display takes place, with more or less vigour, at any time during the day, in April or May, but it is seen at its best very early in the morning, or in the evening. Sometimes morning mist on the moor makes visibility so bad that all is a blank. I remember one May morning starting off in a car at 6.0 a.m. (S.T.). From below we could see that there was heavy mist above the moor, but knowing from past experience that, as sometimes happens, it might prove to be more clear on top, we decided to try our luck. As we slowly ascended through the murk we nearly ran over three stray sheep and innumerable rabbits. But at the trysting-place the mist was impenetrable for more than a few yards. Such conditions, however disappointing for us, evidently did not abate the ardour of the blackcock, for we could hear the curious assortment of noises which accompanies their antics, or even occasionally catch a tantalising glimpse of the actors, but that was all. Fortified by hot coffee, and hope, we waited for an hour, but in vain. The mist scattered momentarily, now and again; but finally settled down more thickly than ever.

A few days later my wife and I tried again: it was a clear summer morning and we settled down to watch from the car before seven o'clock. A blackcock in breeding plumage is a magnificent, almost awe-inspiring spectacle. Head, neck and mantle gleam in sunlight with a rich, purple sheen, against which the scarlet patches of bare skin over and behind the eye, or the white fleck on 'shoulder' show up boldly. When the birds display their appearance is even more splendid. The brown-black wings are drooped sideways, the neck is puffed out and, with the head, extended forwards, while at the same time the tail feathers are raised and spread forwards and sideways till the curved outer quills reach the ground. If there is a strong wind the birds are blown about like sailing boats. And—most striking feature of all—the pure white feathers beneath the tail are opened fanwise and arched forwards, so that viewed from the rear the turkey-cocked tail looks as if its inner surface had been painted white.

The evolutions of the cocks when displaying are extraordinary. Two stalk towards each other uttering weird war-cries, with heads down and tails spread, so that you expect a tournament *à l'outrance* to ensue: but there is no shedding of blood. Facing each other, they jib backwards and forwards as if jerked by elastic. Occasionally a couple will spar but no feathers fly. More often after posturing face to face the *soi-disant* combatants walk away side by side, or subside gradually and begin a preening toilet, subsequently flying off a short distance to feed on whortleberry leaves. The advent of another cock, however, stirs the whole congregation to another exhibition of physical jerks. Simultaneously seven or eight cocks leap upwards spasmodically as though a miniature mine exploded beneath them and the same futile pantomime is repeated. I have read descriptions of blackcock really fighting, beating each other with their wings, on these occasions. I can only say I have never seen a serious conflict on Exmoor.

The sounds which form an accompaniment to these uncouth antics are indescribable. To be appreciated they must be heard. There is a bubbling note recalling the 'gobble' of a turkey-cock or the gurgle of a mountain stream; or as my wife suggested, an embryonic attempt to gargle. Another call, often reiterated for minutes on end, reminds me of the whirring of Manx-shearwaters from their burrows at night, which I have heard in the Isles of Scilly and on Skomer and Skokholm. Its rhythm consists of an accented note followed by a shorter one thrice repeated, the last of the short notes being staccato. The timbre is dove-like, 'condoling', as Bottom would say. It is the whirring note which Sir Hugh Gladstone has likened to the sound of a 'curling stone travelling over keen ice'. Another call is like the spit of an angry cat, or the protest of a leaky soda-water siphon: this sound normally follows the ungainly leaps into the air, above described. But to translate the cacophonies of this jazz-band into prose is a Sisyphean task, and I am only too conscious of my inadequacy. The bubbling note which I have mentioned, I have also heard in September and October; blackcock are said to display at this season, but I have never seen them doing so on Exmoor. Such behaviour has been described as pseudo-erotism.

Though I have watched the display of blackcock many times, it is surprising that I have never seen any grey hens present, and other observers tell me that they have had the same experience. Probably the scarcity on Exmoor of grey hens, alluded to above, is the reason; in May the few which exist are probably sitting on eggs, and, though blackcock are polygamous, many of the displaying cocks must be mateless. Descriptions of what occurs when grey hens are present differ. Miss Frances Pitt found that the grey hens entirely ignored the showing off of the cocks. Edmund Selous, however, relates how he saw the female select the male of her choice and crouch before him. The cock's display when hens are present differs from the postures of bravado before their own sex. As described by Selous, the cock passes the hen first on one side and then on the other, tilting his body sideways and downwards towards her so that she has a full view of his resplendent plumage and scarlet wattle: as he turns his arched, white under-tail feathers are also exhibited before her.

There are other 'lekking' places on Exmoor: one is at the higher end of a strip of grass among heather on Rowbarrow, the hill to the west of Dunkery Beacon. The display can be watched from the Langcombe Head road at a distance of several hundred yards: it is impossible to bring a car nearer.

Blackcock, like big-game, do not seem to object to the presence of a car so long as the occupants are quiet and motionless. Wild creatures are quick to perceive movement but their powers of penetrative sight are comparatively small.

While watching the blackcock's display there will be many pleasant distractions. Ring ousels chatter at you from beech hedges and whinchats warble their sweet, inconsequent songs from gorse clumps. Cuckoos are not popular in avian circles: we saw one mobbed by meadow pipits, carrion crows, magpies and jays, which gave him—or her—a very unpleasant five minutes. And from the Langcombe Head road you look across to Sweetworthy and its bluebells. They creep across the sward, clear of trees but for a few ancient, wind-tortured thorns, like a shimmering veil of pale blue mist. Their tints vary every minute with the mutabilities of light and shade. In bright sunlight they glow turquoise to which the sheen of their glaucous leaves is a foil. A cloud transmutes this to sapphire. Mist, prowling up from the Bristol Channel, gentles sapphire to mauve. Their delicate scent, more subtle than hawthorn or rowan, is borne on the wind. Furled crockets of fern do not as yet hide the flowers, but amid this cerulean ocean are eyots of vivid green grass, inlays of emerald upon turquoise or sapphire. Bluebells, woodland shaded, have a dappled beauty, but it is only on wide open spaces that they reveal such dazzling brilliance.

CHAPTER XVI

PORLOCK MARSH

The Marsh owes its origin to the shingle bank which bars out the Bristol Channel. Tides sweeping to and fro in restless vicissitude have piled up a rampart that at its eastern end is almost a hundred yards in breadth. It was not always so: records reveal that there was an inlet from the Channel, and perhaps a sheet of water, for some four centuries ago cygnets from 'le lac' were brought to the Lady of the Manor. Possibly it was up this inlet that the Danes sailed when they burnt Porlock. Even now the sea sometimes breaks the barrier at its weakest point, and then 'le lac' again comes into being and forms a shining expanse of water half a mile in length.

The best barley in England is grown on the fields fringing the Marsh: their fertility is attributed to the salt water that once covered them; some lie today below sea level. Beyond the shingle bank, more to the west, the stumps of trees are uncovered at low tides: the old men say they can remember when the trees bore branches.

The Marsh consists partly of an expanse of mud and shallow pools intersected by drains and overgrown by rough grass and rushes, and partly of a swamp covered with dense reeds; these in spring and summer have green pennons and whisper delightful folk-tales; in winter their dry stalks rattle and gibber like a skeleton dance.

Inland from the Marsh a rampart of moorland and wooded hills stretches in a gracious curve from the rocky hog's back of Hurlstone Point on the east to the pines of Culbone on the west. Between rise the rounded summit of Bossington Beacon, its feet covered by ilex groves, the heathery knoll called Crawter, the long belt of oak and fir forming 'The Parks' (the ancient hunting ground of Porlock Manor), and the wild moorland, 1400 feet high, of Porlock Common: thus Porlock village and its neighbouring farmland are enclosed in a natural amphitheatre. Towards West Porlock there was once another wood and a duck-decoy: you can still see the remains of its pipes.

The Marsh, though it cannot compete with an estuary in variety, is rich in bird life. Here in March come the first wheatears: nearly all pass through, and are followed by the Greenlanders. To distinguish these from the former is sometimes difficult, but when a party of the latter is seen together the brighter colouring and slightly larger size is obvious. There is a double migration both east and west of swallows along the coast and across the Channel to Wales. On a warm April evening you may find hundreds of them hawking over the pools, or resting on trees. A dead oak, now long since fallen, was at one time a favourite resting place. With them are sandmartins and perhaps a few housemartins. About the same time the yellow wagtails arrive, very often in company with white wagtails, of which you may see as many as a baker's dozen: you can tell them by their pearly-grey mantles. Common sandpipers arrive in April too, and now and again a turnstone in its tortoiseshell spring plumage and knots in their quaker-grey winter dress. One morning a snow bunting perched upon a dry patch in the middle of the Marsh, a curious place to meet with this species, though these buntings are fairly frequent visitors to the higher parts of the moor in hard winters. But all these are passengers and do not breed with us.

The reed-bed in May is peopled by sedge-warblers sliding up and down the stalks with guttural, sibilant chatter, and the rarer marsh warbler has been known to sojourn with them for a while. A few reed-buntings breed here. Some eighteen years ago a pair of nightjars nested on the shingle bank and brought up their young. It was strange to see this denizen of heath and moorland circling over the sea when put up from the shingle. Redshank are always present, noisy and suspicious of intruders, especially when they are anxious over newly hatched young. Once in June I saw a dunlin in breeding plumage join the redshanks and swoop down in the headlong court-ship flight which is usually seen only in their nesting haunts further north. They are always to be found on the Marsh except in the height of the breeding season. Some still retain the black smudge on the belly, which is part of the summer plumage, as late as the last days of August. Their aerial evolutions make even teal seem clumsy fliers: when they turn their white breasts to slanting sunlight they are metamorphosed as if by magic from dun to silver. Now and again you may catch among them a smaller wader, with a light-brown streak from lore to eye; it is a little stint.

Ringed plovers lay their eggs, almost indistinguishable from the pebbles, on the shingle, and perform their weird broken-wing antics when the tiny, freckled young are in danger. Red-backed shrikes are later arrivals: they put together their large untidy nests in derelict hedges, and impale bees, cockchafers and small birds upon the thorns of sloe bushes: a young grass snake several inches long formed part of one larder; a partly incubated red-backed shrike's

egg, found spiked on barbed wire, may have been removed by the
parents from the nest when it did not hatch. But a larder is not always
made; in fact it is the exception rather than the rule, in this locality.

In August returning migrants appear. Common sandpipers and
wheatears are among the first, but with them the returning wagtails
appear again, white and yellow; many of the latter are young birds
with olive mantles. After them come greenshank and green sandpipers. Greenshanks stand much higher in the water than green
sandpipers, and they are stouter in build than redshanks. In a good
light they look very grey and white birds, and the greenish legs and
long black bill are very noticeable; there is a thick, black line down
the rump and tail in flight. Their call note sounds to me 'tchui-tchu-
tchu-tchu', but there is another note, 'teh-teh-teh-'. They often fly
off into the wind and then drift down wind, gliding gracefully over
the Marsh before settling. Miss Frances Pitt's beautiful photograph
shows one at its northern nesting place from which those we see here
are returning. Green sandpipers have a conspicuous white rump and
at a distance the rest of the plumage looks black, but a nearer view
shows that the black is really grey. When disturbed they tower high
in flight, calling 'te-te-teu', a note rather like a redshank's, but if
you keep your glasses on them you will find that almost immediately
they return to the spot where they were originally feeding.

About the same time come the ruffs. They can always be identified
by the black and brown barred feathers of their upper plumage,
which resembles that of a hen pheasant, the slight, white wing-bar
and the dark line dividing the oblong white patches on the rump.
They are often remarkably unafraid of man. Probably they come from
Holland where they are not molested. One evening in September I
went down to the Marsh with a friend who wished to see some
waders. We put up a green sandpiper which flew a few hundred
yards and then settled. I walked towards the spot, intending to drive
the bird back to my friend. When I had gone a short distance two
birds flew towards me, which I at first thought might be whimbrel,
till I noticed that their beaks were straight. They settled only about
twenty yards away from me and then I saw that they were a ruff and
a reeve: as they ran and paddled amidst the small pools and runnels
and the brown grass, they were difficult to follow, and I lost sight of
one of them. The other I shepherded towards my friend: when I
rejoined him he told me that the ruff which I had lost had been
feeding tamely quite near me all the time.

In winter teal, trim, tidy little ducks, are abundant: flocks of over
a hundred are frequent. The black and white lines on the wing, the

rich chestnut and green on the head, the metallic green speculum, and buff patches on the under tail coverts, contrasted with the wavy greys of mantle and flanks, make them look gaudy in bright sunlight. Alert to spy strangers, they spring to flight quickly, and with many a twist and turn swoop seawards over the shingle bank. They do not tower high, as gulls do, but vary their altitude whimsically, feinting to settle and then swerving upwards. I have seen a starling, which attempted to join in their manœuvres, constantly left in the lurch, so quickly do the changes of direction follow each other.

Wigeon, too, come to the Marsh pools, but more often they float in the bay at a safe distance from the shore: I love to hear the call of the drakes, 'whee-òo' on a moonlight night. Shovelers are rarer visitors, but when they do come their broadly painted colours of chestnut, blue and white are a lovely combination. Tufted duck I have seen only on a few occasions, and then usually on the sea in company with teal. Only in hard winters are there many geese: white-fronted are the commonest, but sometimes there are a few brent, and once after severe weather a gaggle of grey-lags remained for a fortnight.

The rare long-tailed duck I have twice seen on the Marsh: both birds were immature males or females, with short, pointed tails and brown patches on the cheeks. Other uncommon visitors are grey phalaropes: they look like miniature gulls, and are full of an amazing vitality, expressed in swift, zig-zag rushes, in search of their prey on the surface of the pools. Once in November I saw a shore-lark on the edge of an inlet which I call 'shore-lark creek'. It was very tame and watched me unconcernedly, perched on a stone, for some minutes: the black gorget and eyestripe were undeveloped, and it had no crest: probably it was a female. And in the same month I was lucky to see two tawny pipits: I was attracted by the tawny colouring of their upper plumage and the celerity with which they ran.

Whimbrel arrive in May on their way north and again on their journey south in August. Curlew are here in hordes in winter and lapwings too. Herons, probably from the heronry at Dulverton on the other side of the moor (they are locally called 'Dulverton men') stalk about the ditches or stand picturesque but wary on the pool's margin. I once saw one sitting on the ground: at a distance it looked like a grey goose. Kingfishers, alert for little fishes, perch on posts by the larger drains, or skim, cobalt and green, above the azure water.

Oyster-catchers are primarily birds of the sea-shore. But one August evening after a severe thunderstorm there was a line of fifty ranged along an island formed in the middle of the Marsh by recent

Opposite: Fledged young ravens in nest

heavy rain. They were very talkative with their 'peet-peet' cries: one
or two would begin and then the rest of the congregation took up
the refrain. When they flew to the side of the Marsh the white cross,
on their upper plumage and upper tail coverts, was striking. This
cross is the origin of a picturesque old Gaelic legend. When Christ
was resting on the sea-shore, and his enemies came in search of
Him, oyster-catchers covered Him with sea-weed and thus foiled his
foes. Ever since then the oyster-catcher carries in flight a white cross
upon his back.

Gulls, who love fresh water to bathe in, resort to the Marsh pools
for this purpose, and rest and preen themselves on the banks. The
black-headed is the most plentiful species, but in winter common
gulls are quite as numerous. Herring gulls come here too and there
are a few of those sinister and voracious fowl, the greater black-
backed. Linnets assemble here in autumn and winter and there are
usually a few pairs of stonechats on the gorse bushes near by.
Chaffinch flocks feed on the flotsam and jetsam after a high tide, and
in hard weather they are joined by bramblings. Common snipe
haunt a patch of reedy tussocks: jack snipe I have flushed but seldom:
they rise silently and make but short flights before settling again.

Merlins at this season leave their moorland haunts and hunt the
Marsh: I watched a hen of this species unsuccessfully harry a meadow
pipit, with many a twist and turn; just in time the quarry found
sanctuary in a briar bush. Peregrines are less frequent aggressors:
ravens croak as they fly overhead but unless a dead sheep is washed
up they are too cunning to descend to earth.

At all seasons the Marsh is lovely, even when its lagoons are
whipped to miniature breakers by bitter north-easters off the Bristol
Channel, or, in contrast, when on a frosty night its glassy waters
reflect the sparkling of the earliest stars. But I most love the Marsh
on an autumn evening, when the wind in the dry reed-stalks is but a
secret whisper and the sky's wistful hues are repeated, blue, silver
and cloudy opal, on unruffled water. A skein of mist, ghost-grey,
floats motionless against swart woodlands, below the knife-edge of
the moor: pillars of ashen smoke rise unwavering above brown roofs:
a film of haze dims even the whiteness of cottage walls: curlew fly
over crooning sweetly. And from the woods inland comes the
'belling' of red stags, a cry in which passion and pain are mingled.

Opposite: (above) Young ravens, a few days old, in nest
(below) Young ravens, close-up of gape. Raven's nest and eggs

I

CHAPTER XVII

EXCITEMENTS OF AN EXMOOR BIRDWATCHER

Bird-watching is, I believe, considered to be a mild form of lunacy, by some full-blooded people. At any rate, the bird-watcher, if not necessary, is harmless, provided he does not steal eggs; and, being usually a modest man, he does not bore his friends, after the manner of the golf maniac, by relating his experiences, unless wantonly provoked to do so.

His pursuit has infinite variety: there are always new thrills. For instance, he may catch a bird which he knows well behaving in an unusual manner. The peregrine's stoop I have often seen, but one day on the coast near Porlock I saw the falcon perform a thirty-foot nose-dive, turn over on her back, glide thus a short distance, reverse to the original position, and continue her headlong descent. Then she 'threw-up' and sailed away over a rocky promontory out of sight. With ravens this trick is a commonplace; this peregrine must have had frequent opportunities of seeing the ravens' acrobatics, for they are near neighbours and ancient enemies. Perhaps she was proving to her own satisfaction that she could manage an aerial tumble as well as any clumsy, big, black bird, or perhaps it was simply exuberance. But I have never seen or heard of a peregrine behaving in this way before.

Another bird-watching excitement is the observation at close quarters of birds which do not often allow a near approach. One November day there was a tapping on the split larch fence outside our back windows, which seemed too uninterrupted to be caused by a great tit. At first we could see nothing, but in a minute or two a cock lesser-spotted (or barred) woodpecker flitted from behind a buddleia bush and flattened himself against the dark-reddish bark of a larch pole. Evidently this post was full of larvae, for the bird travelled up and down it for about ten minutes, hammering at it with his pick-axe bill, and at times throwing back his head while he swallowed his prey.

Now and again we could see his long tongue flick out to secure his victim: sometimes he extracted a delicacy by inserting the tip of his beak in a hole and twisting his head round in an almost spiral movement. Occasionally he chipped off bits of bark. Descending the pole, he proceeded by clumsy hops, tail foremost. On inspecting the post after he had departed, I found it pitted with holes, some of which were fresh, and had evidently been pecked out by him, while others were the old borings of insects.

Later he climbed to the top of one of the larch poles in the fence, and hung with his front toes grasping the edge and his breast resting on its flat surface. There he preened himself, scratching his chin and breast, stretching out his wings and combing them and spreading his tail. Once he yawned—or tried to eject a pellet—but nothing came of it. Perched thus he looked the quaintest little bundle of feathers.

Another year a hen lesser-spotted woodpecker visited the same fence. Her behaviour was much the same as that of the cock. We noticed that the long, snaky back claw was held out almost at right angles as she climbed. A fence of split larch poles must, to a woodpecker, seem a labour-saving wood, where food is available with the least possible exertion: you can hop or crawl from one bole to the next.

Seen from behind, the plumage of the barred woodpecker curiously resembles the white ash and black cracks on the surface of a charred log. It is this chequered colouring which is so protective when the bird is stationary on a birch truck, for there, too, the bars on its back assimilate with the horizontal fissures on the tree's bright-coloured surface. There are shades of red, also, on the birch's bole which harmonize with the faint reddish tinge on this woodpecker's breast, and do not clash with the scarlet on its forehead. On the dull russet surface of larch poles these colours were even more protective.

On another occasion in April my wife and I watched a cock lesser-spotted woodpecker feeding on the flowers of an ash in Horner Woods. I had never before seen this bird behaving in this manner and I do not know whether he was extracting insects from the flowers or consuming the yellow pistils or purple stamens. His proceedings were more typical of a tit than a woodpecker, for he usually hung suspended beneath the swaying branches.

The controversy as to whether the drumming of woodpeckers is vocal or instrumental recurs at intervals. Neither of the woodpeckers drummed on our fence, but I have been fortunate enough to watch them drumming in the woods at close quarters for many hours. One morning in May a cock lesser-spotted flew over my head in Rey Coombe, near Porlock, and settled on a dead, rotten branch of an oak twenty yards away from me. It first drummed about half-way along the branch, which was roughly six feet long, and then almost at its extremity. The middle of the branch was thicker than the end, and it was clear that the noise produced on the thicker wood was deeper and lower in pitch than when the drumming took place near the branch's tip: on the thinner wood the sound was thinner and sharper in tone. He then flew to another dead branch of about the same length, near the first one and on the same tree, and drummed again with exactly the same results: the thicker wood produced a deeper, and the thinner wood a more tenuous, scrannel note.

I also observed that the violence of the blows affected the volume of sound: the resonance diminished with softer blows. The head was blurred during the drumming. The bird remained at the end of the second branch, drumming at intervals, for about a minute. The beak appeared to me to be closed, and I watched the whole operation with field-glasses. When the bird pecked, but did not 'drum', on a different branch shortly afterwards, only a very small sound was produced, and the pecks were made deliberately, not quickly. I examined the branches on which he had drummed and could see no beak-marks on them: rapid, vibratory blows would not mark the wood. The duration of each drumming was about two seconds, and the intervals between each performance usually three seconds, but sometimes as long as six seconds. On two occasions soon after I again watched the male and also the female lesser-spotted woodpeckers drumming, and again noticed the same differences in pitch corresponding with the thickness or thinness of the dead branch. When the hen drummed the duration was shorter than when the cock performed: again the beak appeared to me to be closed.

Some ornithologists hold that the drumming of woodpeckers is vocal, produced by the bird's throat, and not instrumental. My own observations lead me to the conclusion that the sound is entirely instrumental, the result of the vibration caused by the hammering of the bird's beak upon dead or rotten wood. The differences in tone, volume and pitch which occur according to the thickness or thinness of the wood, are significant, and to my mind conclusive.

If there were any vocal element in drumming then, since the vibratory sound varies with the consistency of the wood, the vocal element must be constant. But when the vibratory note is most tenuous, i.e. where the wood is thinnest, no vocal sound can be distinguished.

Again, if drumming is a song, vocal and not instrumental, why does a woodpecker find it necessary when 'singing' to move its head so rapidly that it becomes a blur? Does the same phenomenon occur in connection with the song of any other bird? When the nightjar churrs or the grasshopper warbler reels or the cirl bunting 'sizzles' this blurring does not occur. Is not the natural inference that the blurred head of the drumming woodpecker is connected not with song but with rapid vibratory blows?

While watching these birds, and while listening to them drumming when they are not visible, I endeavoured to count the number of blows given during each spell. I found that the separate taps in each drumming vary between nine and eleven. The hen which I saw drumming did not exceed eight taps; unseen birds drumming often did not reach ten and never exceeded eleven strokes. One of the cocks scratched his head between bouts of hammering, and the rate at which he scratched seemed much the same as when he drummed. Drumming usually begins softly but swells to a crescendo.

Another of the bird-watcher's excitements is the unexpected appearance of a rare bird. One morning late in September Mr. A. V. Cornish, of Minehead, telephoned that a bird of a very rare species had been seen on the Golf Links. I went there in the afternoon and met Mr. Cornish; he told me that the groundsman had also seen the bird in the morning but though we walked the whole length of the Links we failed to see it. Returning, we met the groundsman, and while we were talking to him Mr. Cornish sighted the bird flying towards us from the shore. It passed high over our heads and I kept my field-glasses on it until it was out of sight. It flew strongly, with many twists and turns, like those of a snipe, but less rapid. The only colour I could distinguish was a sandy-fawn on its mantle. But as we walked back, about ten minutes later, Mr. Cornish spotted the bird on the ground not fifty yards away. We approached within thirty yards of it, and had a most excellent view, for it was very tame. Its size was about that of a golden plover: its general colouring was sand-brown, and its long legs in strong sunlight looked a very light grey, almost white. The large head recalled a stone curlew, but from the prominent black 'boot-button' eye a black eye-stripe ran backwards, with a parallel white stripe above the black. Seen from the behind the black and white stripes formed a triangle enclosing a very lovely lavender patch at the back of the head. The black beak was decurved: the breast pale fawn.

It was a delicate, dainty little bird, and ran swiftly with little mincing steps. When, shortly after, it flew again, I saw the black tips to its wing quills and the white edges to its tail feathers. The only notes I heard were a short 'grut', or 'wuk', and 'tchit-tchit' before taking to flight. There could be no doubt as to its identity: it was a Cream Coloured Courser, a bird of which there are only about twenty-four recorded appearances in England.

The next day I saw the bird again in the same place and watched it for nearly two hours. Its posture as it stands facing you is very upright, with neck erect and legs straightened, but after making each short run in search of food it spasmodically depresses the whole of its body so that its very short tail touches the ground, and the legs are bent almost double at the 'knee'; at the same time the neck shoots upwards. This extraordinary action is so violent that it suggests 'physical jerks': it reminded me of the blow from the shoulders dealt by a nuthatch when hammering a nut, but at a slower pace.

Occasionally it preened itself between the shoulders, the wind ruffling up its brown mantle, and combed its outstretched wing with its claw. When it flapped its wings its black axillaries were so much in evidence that it was momentarily transfigured from a brown to a black bird.

While I was watching, a peregrine, from its size a falcon, flew over. The Courser was at the time screened from my view by a bunker, but directly afterwards I found it crouched on the ground as though sitting on eggs, but with head erect, not depressed. It remained in this posture for ten minutes.

I could not see on what it was feeding, but once it had in its beak a black object which may have been a leather jacket. Crane flies were all over the Links, but it did not take them even when they pitched near it. It was difficult to put the bird up: when I approached it it ran swiftly but did not fly.

It was delightful to have so fine a view of this rare bird for so long, and again in bright sunlight. Its sleek plumage, mincing gait, tameness and charming traits of behaviour made the whole incident memorable.

In Vol. IV of the new *Handbook of British Birds* the legs are described as milk-white, but the plate shows them as yellowish. Coward, in Vol. III of the *Birds of the British Isles*, says that the legs of birds in captivity were distinctly yellow. The legs of the bird I watched had no yellowish tinge about them. Howard Saunders describes them as white with an enamelled appearance.

It would be interesting to know how this bird, whose habitat abroad is N. Africa and S.W. Asia, reached West Somerset. I was lucky to spend so much time in its company. It was seen again the next day by Mr. G. F. Luttrell, but not afterwards.

While shooting near Dunster in December 1938, Mr. G. F. Luttrell saw a woodpecker, whose colour was black; it flew past him so near that he could have shot it. I have little doubt that it was a black woodpecker, a continental species. Detailed evidence was given in *The Field* in March 1936 of its identification in Great Britain by several competent observers. Nevertheless scientific ornithologists refuse to allow this bird a niche in the British list. It is stated that caged specimens have been released on at least one occasion. But if every record of a rarity is to be received with derisive incredulity unless the corpse is produced for the pundits to gloat over, bird-watchers will cease to think it worth while to report uncommon birds. Already the illegal activities of collectors make it dangerous to give recent data for rare or uncommon species. So long as scientific ornithologists preserve an intransigent attitude as regards authentic reports of 'unprocured' specimens ornithology will continue to suffer.

I know of two other instances where good records have been summarily rejected. A white-winged lark was clearly identified both as to plumage and notes by a friend of mine who is an excellent field-naturalist and has a trained musical ear. Another friend, a most reliable observer, saw at close quarters and sketched an aquatic warbler. But both these identifications were rejected for reasons which seemed inadequate. That fine naturalist, the late T. A. Coward, a good friend to me and many another bird-lover, took a broader view. He insisted on precise and accurate descriptions, but when convinced gave unstinted appreciation.

After all the question whether the record is 'accepted' or not cannot affect the aesthetic pleasure of the sight of a rare and beautiful bird. It is enshrined in the treasury of the mind where none can smirch its beauty. And the same applies to a doubtful identification: last autumn I saw among a flock of skylarks a lark which answered in some respects to the description of a white-winged lark. I failed to get a closer view, nor did I ever come upon the bird again. But the possibility of having seen so uncommon a migrant was a joy which nothing can liquidate.

It is always an exciting moment when you see a bird in unexpected surroundings. Watching starlings feeding on the lawn from my study window one December morning I was surprised to find a woodcock among them. It probed amid worm-casts for a minute and then disappeared in bat-like flight over the south hedge. Another day a greenfinch which seemed smaller than the rest resolved itself into a cock siskin in good plumage, with dark cap and bib. It flew from the lawn to the bird-table just outside the window and fed there quite tamely for several minutes. Then it dropped down to the edge of the bird-bath and sipped: a dainty sight.

Though of late years ravens have been allowed in some sparsely populated districts to revert to their ancient habit of nesting in trees, to see a tree nest is a rather unusual experience. I have seen several in the last ten years. The quest for one of them was very nearly fruitless. The old birds were flying about over the wood, in a frantic state of excitement, continually crying 'uk, uk', the warning note to the young. We watched them for a couple of hours, but they gave no clue and baffled us entirely.

We were making a final search, before giving up, when I noticed a nest about forty feet up in a tall spruce near the edge of a rather sparse strip of woodland. Beating upon the trunk with a stick produced answering squawks which showed that the nest was tenanted. The spruce was quite unclimbable by me, but there was a Scots fir near, up which I clambered: thence I could see that the nest contained three young ravens, probably about ten days old, and a villainous basketful of young ruffians they looked. This site has now been abandoned.

Another tree raven's nest my wife and I discovered when looking for a different quarry. As we turned up a moorland coombe a raven flew over from the north uttering that strange call which resembles a distant motor horn. Soon after two more ravens appeared, evidently, from the variety of their notes, in a great state of excitement: they 'drew corks', and clucked 'uk, uk', and the male, the smaller of the two, did side-slip dives. They always kept near a subsidiary coombe, and on approaching this we could see a large untidy nest in an ivied tree. Not wishing to disturb the birds or call attention to the nest by nailmarks on the trunk, I did not climb the tree, which was quite an easy one. But by ascending the steep bank of the goyal I could see eggs in the nest; it was deeply lined with wool.

I returned to the place about a fortnight later, climbed the tree and found three unfledged, blind young in the nest. My next visit was after the interval of another fortnight. I found the nest empty and bootmarks on the trunk. I fear the young had come to a bad end.

The following year I was told of another tree raven's nest a mile or two from last year's site. By this time the nestlings had safely flown; the old birds and at least three young were in the air together. The nest was in the crotch of an oak about fifty feet from the ground.

The next spring news came of a raven's nest in a dead tree, in a new locality. The valley to which my wife and I were directed wound tortuously upwards. Soon the valley divided: my wife took the left, I the right defile. As I rounded a shoulder which blocked my view upwards I saw the nest, a bulky bundle of sticks in the fork of a dead ash some fifty feet from the ground. The site was a typical instance of raven cunning, for the tree was quite invisible from the lower part of the coombe.

On my approach the old ravens produced a complete vocabulary of corvine abuse. The hen, the larger of the pair, perched above the nest and gave vent to her maternal rage by ripping off clots of moss and bark from the branches. Her spouse kept a safe distance. The nestlings awoke with peevish hunger cries. From the hillside I could look down upon the nest and its four young ravens in grey feathers probably about a fortnight old.

My wife and I watched these interesting young hooligans while their parents cursed us heartily. When finally we descended, the old hen wished us every evil chance on our homeward way, a sinister silhouette on the skyline.

A few days later I visited the valley again. At the foot of the tree lay most of the nest and the corpses of four young ravens almost fully fledged. Enquiries showed that all was well at half-past eight one night but by six-thirty next morning the nest and its occupants had been destroyed by unknown marauders. The episode shows how hard is the struggle for existence for our rarer birds.

All the tree ravens' nests which I have seen were built in the crotch of a tree at or near the head of a valley, whence there was a broad and spacious prospect over the surrounding country: ravens wish to be able to spy strangers at a distance.

To hear a jay sing for the first time is an adventure. It happened in a larch-wood near Horner Mill. The notes resembled the well-known 'pee-ou' of a buzzard, but their timbre was even more querulous and plaintive, and the phrases were continuous, one following another in quick succession. Montagu mentions a jay imitating the 'song' of a buzzard and Bewick was once led to suspect the village carpenter of Sabbath breaking because a jay imitated so well the rasping sound of a saw.

Judging from his cacophonous cries you would hardly expect the jay to have a pleasing song: it would seem more likely to deserve S. T. Coleridge's well-known epigram:—

> *Swans sing before they die—'twere no bad thing*
> *Should certain persons die before they sing.*

Nevertheless its song is, or can be, quite musical and melodious. Hudson's experience was that the same notes and phrases were not ordinarily heard in any two localities, and that the bird was able to emit a great variety of sounds—some highly musical. He adds that the jay also has a real song, and that this singing of the jay is some-what of a puzzle, as it is not the same song in any two places; it gives one the idea that there is no traditional song in this species, but that each bird that has a song has invented it for himself. It varies from a soft chatter and warble, just audible at a distance of thirty or forty yards, to a song composed of several musical notes harmoniously arranged, which may be heard distinctly a quarter of a mile away. This set and far-reaching song is rare.

Some years ago I mentioned the jay's powers of mimicry in an article published in a periodical. Shortly afterwards a Bristol correspondent wrote in a local paper that some sixty years ago he kept a tame jay, in a cage, and also a female cat; she had acquaintances whose foregatherings were sometimes 'musical'. In a few months there was not a phrase in all their hideous minstrelsy which the jay could not reproduce with marvellous exactitude. Mercifully the performance was usually given in subdued tones. He would croon himself to sleep by rehearsing the contents of his repertoire in *diminuendo*!

One morning in April I went down to Porlock Marsh, which borders Porlock Bay, to look for migrants. It was a joy to find a flock of yellow wagtails, feeding on a field near the principal stretch of water. I counted them several times, and there were not less than fifty; to watch these dainty little birds, prinked out in saffron yellow, scurrying over the bright green pasture in and out and among the sheep, and now and again taking wing in aerial curvettes, all in brilliant sunshine, blue sky and white-sailed clouds above and azure water beyond, was an enchanting experience. Nor was this all: there was one wagtail which differed slightly in plumage and in behaviour from the rest: sometimes it mingled with the flock, but sometimes fed apart. It was a blue-headed wagtail. Its pale blue head, forehead and nape, white eyestripe and chin, golden breast and olive mantle made identification certain. Probably, from the brightness of its colouring, it was a male. Curiously enough, the only other blue-headed wagtail I have ever seen in this district was one at Minehead just seven years before, to the day. All wagtails are delightful to watch: they have such delicately whimsical ways. The grey and the yellow are the most beautiful, but it is only the yellows that you see in flocks in my country. In sunlight they are brilliant as a bevy of dandelions: their plumage is luminous. I count this flock and their rare companion among the most delightful of my bird-watching excitements. The memory recurs to me, as did Wordsworth's daffodils to him.

CHAPTER XVIII

THE KINDLY INFLUENCE OF BIRDS

In *The Little Flowers of St. Francis of Assisi* we are told, in the famous story of the saint preaching to the birds, that he 'rejoiced with them, and was glad and marvelled much at so great a company of birds and their most beautiful diversity and their good heed and sweet friendliness, for the which cause he devoutly praised their Creator in them'.

And another of the 'Little Flowers' tells how he begged a young man, who had caught many turtle doves and was carrying them for sale, to give them to him so that they 'might not fall into the hands of cruel men that would kill them'. The young man gave St. Francis the birds, and 'he went and made nests for them all: and they abiding therein, began to lay their eggs and hatch them before the eyes of the brothers: and so tame were they, they dwelt with St. Francis and all the other brothers as though they had been fowls that had always fed from their hands'. And the young man 'became a brother and lived in the Order in great sanctity'.

To me, a bird-lover, these legends of St. Francis make as strong an appeal as any of his good works, for they bring him very near to me across the centuries, even if their ornithology will not stand too critical an examination. The first story is entirely consonant with all we know of the Saint's lovable character; the second is a telling example of how the love of birds has a humanising influence over unregenerate human nature.

It is a little curious that these legends should have grown up around an Italian. In their preface to that entrancing book *Why Birds Sing*, by M. Jacques Delamain, the well-known French naturalist, M. M. Jerome and Jean Tharaud write: 'The Anglo-Saxon race, and in a more general fashion, the Protestant races, are infinitely more interested in all this winged world than the Catholic Latins. . . . A mystic like St. Francis of Assisi . . . is only an exception to the rule.' And they add that they are 'not surprised that he should be about the only one among the saints to have captivated the Protestant mind'.

Certainly the Latin races have not hitherto enjoyed a good reputation for kindness to birds or animals. Readers of *The Story of San Michele* will remember Dr. Axel Munthe's struggle to stop the blinding of quails on Monte Barbarossa, and how in the end he was able to force the owner to sell him the property so that he might make it a bird sanctuary. In France the 'chasseur' shoots every small bird for the pot; it is to be hoped that in time *la Ligue Française pour la Protection des Oiseaux* will put a stop to his depredations.

Among other continental nations there exists—or did before the War—a more humane attitude towards bird life. The transportation by aeroplane to Italy of swallows overcome by cold in Germany and Austria is a memorable instance. In Switzerland there are several bird protection societies. The English-speaking races have a good record: many wild life and bird sanctuaries exist in our colonies and mandated territories. America has her National Association of Audubon Societies. A Migratory Birds Convention was completed between the United States and Canada in 1917, which, on paper at any rate, gives protection to many migratory birds, though from the criticisms made by Mr. H. J. Parham in his book *A Nature Lover in British Columbia* it seems that the administration of the law still leaves much to be desired. In Great Britain we have many societies among whose objects are the better protection of bird-life. The Scottish Society for the Protection of Wild Birds proclaims that its aim is 'to make Scotland the most bird-loving country in the world'. 'Grey Owl', with his teaching of tolerance of man towards animals, was another sign of the times, and he loved birds as dearly as he loved his beavers.

All these activities are signs of increasing sympathy for birds and therefore of their kindly influence upon human nature. But it is here in England that these traits are most remarkable: my own experiences, which have, no doubt, been shared by many, seem to illustrate my point. Of the 'sweet friendliness' of some birds in my own garden I have written in another chapter. And from their example their youngsters learn that our house and its environs form an oasis of safety, where food, drink and baths may always be obtained.

And our love of birds is evidently an infectious complaint, for our neighbours have learned its fascination: they have bird-tables, and some of them nesting boxes as well. In fact, all the adjoining gardens are bird-sanctuaries, and the tameness of the bird population in our lane is becoming proverbial in the village: the tamest chaffinches mob passers-by in the expectation that they, like us, carry food about in their pockets for their pleasure.

Wounded birds are often brought to me. When I lived in the North a farmer sent me an injured kestrel which had been shot and afterwards caught by a dog: it lived two months in my greenhouse, the only safe place then available, and had become extraordinary tame by the time I released it. Here, at Porlock, the wire cage which covers my small fruit is a bird-sanatorium.

These straws show which way the wind blows; the growing kindliness towards birds which they reveal is symptomatic of a changed attitude in this country: fifty years ago the few who took any interest in wild birds cared only to keep them in cages or collect their eggs. These atavistic hobbies still persist, but they are, as regards many species, illegal, and their unpopularity is increasing. To most people a bird in the bush is now worth more than two in the hand, for the former is in its natural environment while the latter are either corpses or prisoners.

In the *Life and Letters of John Galsworthy* (Marrott) there is a letter by Galsworthy to a man who had caged a hawk which had pursued a sparrow into his house, from which the following is an extract:—

'I beg you most earnestly to reflect on what captivity means to a hawk or any of the large soaring birds. To keep such a bird caged is to keep on one's premises a piece of solid permanent suffering. . . . Watching the eagles and hawks in our Zoo, where, of course, they have a maximum of freedom and company as compared with private caging, I have often thought what living tragedies they looked. When one reflects on the nature of his (i.e. a hawk's) existence, the huge spaces that he covers, the way his eye is only fitted, as it were, for seeing at vast distances, the more one is forced to the conception of the utter misery he must suffer in a cage. It is as if some demon, for no reason that we can fathom, had seized one of us and shut us away from all the elements of our natural existence, pinned one of us down to perpetual suffering without rhyme or sense—this is what captivity must seem to a hawk.'

I must confess that my own feelings as to the larger *raptores* in Zoos are similar. To see them thus confined gives me no pleasure. It is different when they are captured and trained for hawking, which is their natural bent. There is, of course, no cruelty in a hawk killing for food, any more than in a thrush devouring a worm or a blue tit picking green-fly off rose leaves. They are merely following their instinctive modes of getting a livelihood.

I believe that the waterfowl in St. James's Park have done much to make bird-watching popular and advertise its charms to the public. (They are a boon to the ornithologist too, who elsewhere knows them only at the end of a telescope.) They owe their introduction to Charles II, and that deed, at any rate, must be accounted to him for righteousness. To find birds as wild as mallard, wigeon, tufted duck and coot taking bits of currant bun from your fingers is a liberal education. And the interest shown in the pigeons in Trafalgar Square, at the Bank, in the Parks and at other frequented places in London, is significant. And among sportsmen who shoot game birds I have many friends who have learned to know and love wild birds also.

Though the birds-nesting boy is still a menace, school children are, as a race, more kindly in their feelings towards birds than they were when I was young. I am sure that the Bird and Tree Scheme, organised by the Society for the Protection of Birds, has had a salutary influence: each child chooses a bird and a tree for observation during the whole of a year, and at the end of the period writes an essay upon them. I have read a good many of these essays, and the knowledge and love of bird-life which they reveal is very heartening. These children will never lose the affection for birds which they have learnt at this susceptible age.

It may seem to some that these facts are trivial, and have small significance today when cruelty and injustice have brought about a state of affairs in which civilised nations are killing each other by the most ingeniously scientific methods and when the barbarities of warfare make us sometimes doubt whether the spirit of man has made any real progress since the stone age. But sooner or later the world will return to sanity. Cruelty and injustice bear in themselves the seeds of their own decay; the brutal tyrannies, which now oppress so large a portion of the earth will perish as other tyrannies have perished. Meanwhile let us not forget the humanities. Love, the 'onlie begetter' of gentleness and kindliness, is eternal. It is the feelings of individuals which, in the end, form the national conscience. Those who have learned to love our 'little sisters the birds', as St. Francis called them, and their 'sweet friendliness', are on the side of the angels. In calmer days their influence will count.

In his delightful book, *A Bird in the Bush*, Lord Kennet says: 'To seek the company of birds from time to time . . . is an instinctive search for healing from the wounds of civilisation.' Who feels that has got at the heart of a bird; he knows, to use Lord Kennet's own words, 'the healing in birds' wings.'

In these turbulent times let us remember that:—

> *I come in the little things,*
> *Saith the Lord :*
> *Yea! On the glancing wings*
> *Of eager birds . . .*

On every nest
Where feathery Patience is content to brood
And leaves her pleasure for the high emprize
Of motherhood—
There doth My Godhead rest.[1]

[1] From *Immanence* by Evelyn Underhill.

CHAPTER XIX

AUTUMN BIRD-SONG ON EXMOOR

It has rained consistently all this October day; it quite often does on Exmoor; and yet this morning the woodlark sang continuously, in spite of the deluge. Every morning since 18th September, rain or fine, he has made melody.

The autumn song of birds is a controversial subject among ornithologists. Bird-song wanes in June, and decreases in July, until in August there are few singers. But in September and October there is a reawakening of this delightful music, though only among certain species. Why is this so? The woodlark usually stops singing in June or July. Only twice have I heard his song in August, on the 4th and 22nd. He starts again usually between the 5th and 18th September but sometimes not until October. He warbles intermittently throughout the winter when the temperature is mild, but November is often a songless month.

The cirl bunting is another autumn singer; in fact, like the woodlark, he sings all the year round; I heard one sing in August only an hour or two after his nestlings had been killed by a stoat. The robin's music cheers us in autumn and winter, and in any weather. He croons quietly to himself even in the sultry noons of July and August. Both song and mistle thrush are irregular songsters in winter; I have heard their strains in every month of the year.

The ring-dove, or wood-pigeon, sometimes coos his 'Take *two* cows, David, take' in September, and even in December. Thrice only have I heard a blackbird's song in winter—on 11th and 22nd December and 9th January. Nothing can curb a wren's exuberance; he will cock his tail and burst forth into a ringing peal, which makes his tiny form tremble, in autumn, or on a frosty December morning, or in the midst of the surliest November fog. The dunnock, too, sings in November and December.

The dipper's song I have heard to perfection in December: as I watched him perched on a boulder in the midst of Horner Water I could see his throat throb with melody; his heart was in his song. The great tit begins its 'saw' note in December, and before Xmas you can hear starlings 'charming' at dusk on a mild evening. Green woodpeckers chuckle with exultant laughter in the dusk before winter sunrises, and the lesser-spotted woodpecker sometimes drums as early as New Year's Day.

Willow-warblers sometimes prolong their songs into September but I have never caught a garden warbler making music after July 11th and even then he is husky. (The willow wren's strain is trickling water: the garden warbler's a rushing rill.) Blackcaps usually stop singing early in July: sometimes they winter with us in West Somerset but do not so far as I am aware sing at that time.[1] Chiff-chaffs constantly chime in September and sometimes in October. I have written of chaffinches autumn and winter songs in an earlier chapter.

These are the facts. But why do birds sing at all? In Lord Grey of Fallodon's book, *The Charm of Birds*, there is an imaginary but whimsical dialogue. *A* states the theory that birds sing when food is abundant and vitality high. *B* replies that in August and September when food is particularly abundant, there is least song. *A* returns the shuttle-cock by pointing out that birds, and particularly the males, are then exhausted by the reproduction of their species, and by the moult, and have not recovered sufficiently to be able to sing. But, replies *B*, why then does the thrush sing in October, but not the blackbird? *A* suggests that the blackbird's moult is the more severe, but admits he cannot prove it. *B* then quotes the robin's August song, although his summer moult is drastic. If food and warmth are the decisive factors in song, why does the mistle thrush sing in winter?

And so on, very pleasantly. Lord Grey sums up by saying that though food is essential to song it does not cause it: that courtship and 'territorial sense' are causes of song, but that sometimes birds sing simply from a sense of well-being. I believe that the exponents of the territorial theory try to prove too much. Watch a wood-warbler 'reeling', or fluting his 'dear, dear, dear' among the tree tops, or planing down into the fern; his tiny leaf-green frame quivers and thrills with emotion; or a song thrush, a wren or a chaffinch, in fact any spring songster. The effect of his song may be to warn off trespassers on his demesne, but can any real bird-lover believe that the songster is conscious of anything else but his own intense ecstasy, the joy of the spring in his blood? Some scientific devotees of the territorial theory seem myopic as to the aesthetic element in bird-life. I think that song in some cases is the relief of pent-up emotions. For instance, a wren which I had unwittingly imprisoned in my tool shed, perched on a post and shouted robustiously when released.

[1] Mr. W. L. Colyer tells me that on November 28th, 1943, he heard a black-cap at Sidmouth sing twice, a loud, clear warbling song, of normal pattern but without the usual end notes.

K

And Dr. Eagle Clarke records that skylarks, attracted to the lantern of Eddystone Lighthouse, sang a few notes.

How far do these explanations apply to autumnal and winter song? Perhaps, as M. Delamain says in *Why Birds Sing*, the amorous impulse, which may be slumbering, but is never quite absent, awakens.

My own theory is that after the moulting depression has passed the spring sexual impulse is aroused in autumn and winter by favourable climatic conditions, but that the shortening hours of daylight check this urge, and may, if severe weather coincides, especially high wind from the north or east, put a stop to it altogether for the time being. It is significant that song waxes soon after the shortest day has passed. Professor Rowan, of the University of Alberta, has shown by a series of experiments on captive juncos, an American migratory species, that daylight is for them the primary stimulus to migration. In those birds which were kept in aviaries artificially lighted for gradually increasing periods during winter, the sex organs were developed to the same extent as in spring; in those not subjected to artificial light the sex organs diminished in a normal manner. The first class, when released, disappeared, presumably on migration; the second class remained behind. If length of light, by developing the sex organs, stimulates migration, it would equally stimulate song.

Or, again, autumn and winter song may be with some species partly territorial. In the breeding season song is probably both territorial and amorous. But with the robin, who outside the time of courtship and nesting will not tolerate another of his own species anywhere near him, it must in autumn be partly territorial, though there is pure enjoyment in it also. With the woodlark, too, it may be in part territorial. Lord Grey suspects that the wren's song is, in the same way, connected with territory.

There seems to be only meagre information about the songs of our summer migrants in their winter quarters. Professor Julian Huxley writes in *Bird Watching and Bird Behaviour* that he heard a willow-warbler sing near Lake Nyanza in December. My friend, Major W. Murray Marsden, also heard a willow-warbler in full song in February in Cape Province E., S. Africa. Dr. A. Landsborough Thomson, in *Problems of Bird-migration* mentions that birds of the same species were heard singing feebly on the Congo in October. A correspondent some years ago wrote in the *Spectator* that in Southern Nigeria she heard and saw a nightingale singing in December. Such song can hardly be related to courtship. It may be territorial or pure happiness; perhaps both.

Song evidently expresses various emotions. But, listening to a woodlark on a fine October morning, when the wind is gentled, 'and all over upland and lowland the charm of the golden rod,' I recall Ford's lines:—

> Far better 'tis
> To bless the sun than reason why it shines.

As Lord Grey puts it: 'Perhaps the conclusion of the whole matter is that we should enjoy the song of birds without questioning too closely why they sing. Enjoyment may be impaired by teasing one-self with trying to understand.'

CHAPTER XX

DOES THE ADDER SWALLOW HER YOUNG?

The ancient controversy as to whether the female adder swallows her young (not *se offendendo*, as Hamlet's gravedigger would have it), but in order to protect them from danger, revives periodically. The problem is still unsolved though it is at least as old as Gilbert White.

The *Natural History of Selborne* contains his letter to Pennant (dated June 18th, 1768) in which he wrote:

'Several intelligent folks assure me that they have seen the viper open her mouth, and admit her helpless young down her throat on sudden surprises, just as the female opossum does her brood into the pouch under her belly upon the like emergencies; and yet the London viper-catchers insist on it, to Mr. Barrington, that no such thing ever happens.'

In a letter to Daines Barrington, dated April 29th, 1776, he describes how, in the previous August, he killed and cut open a female viper and found fifteen live young in her belly. The letter ends:

'There was little room to suppose that this brood had ever been in the open air before; and that they were taken in for refuge, at the mouth of the dam, when she perceived that danger was approaching; because then probably we should have found them somewhere in the neck, and not in the abdomen.'

These quotations present the two opposing views in the controversy. There are on record numerous circumstantial accounts given by eye-witnesses. These reports do not greatly vary: the adder was heard hissing; the young ones were seen all round her; she raised her head a little above the ground and the young crawled into her mouth and disapeared. Some witnesses saw the tail of a young adder curling round its mother's jaws. Often they killed the reptile and squeezed the young out of her mouth, or found the fry alive inside her.

So much for the evidence on this side. Now listen to the other. First, it must be remembered that the oviduct of the female adder extends some two thirds of her length, towards the head, so that it is quite possible for the unborn young to be forced out of the mother's mouth, if, as often happens, her body has been shattered by shot or battered by a stick; for the female adder, unlike the grass snake, does not lay eggs, but brings forth her young alive. And further, though the late Mr. Tegetmeier, through *The Field*, offered many years ago a prize of £5 for the production of convincing evidence that female adders swallowed their young, the prize was never won. On 20th October 1927 *The Field* published a short article which stated that one applicant, who wrote that he had seen the last of the brood disappear down its mother's throat, killed the reptile, tied a noose round its neck to prevent the young escaping, and sent it to Dr. Gunther, the then keeper of the Zoological Department of the British Museum. Dr. Gunther dissected it in the presence of the Fellows of the Linnean Society. The stomach of the viper contained a recently swallowed field mouse! Indeed, a *ridiculus mus*! Its tail had been mistaken for that of a young adder. I am not aware of any later expert pronouncement on the point but I believe that there is as yet no *scientific* proof that the adder swallows her young.

How, then, can the evidence of so many eye-witnesses of this phenomenon be explained away? One theory is that the supposed swallowing is an optical illusion. The young wriggle towards the mother and endeavour to conceal themselves underneath the folds of her body: the open jaws of the hissing snake and the celerity of the movements of the youngsters create the illusion that they are being swallowed, whereas really they have disappeared into the maternal coils. In fact, the adder performs an involuntary conjuring trick which the human eye cannot follow. Another suggestion is that what has been seen is an act, perhaps occasional, of cannibalism.

I have also seen it objected that it is physically impossible for an adder to swallow her young. I think this objection cuts no ice. Snakes have no breast or collar bones: the ribs, being free at the ends, can be flattened out to allow distention of the body when the prey is swallowed. The bones of the skull, too, are connected so loosely that the head can be widened, so much so that it is stated that the mouth can admit an object three times the size of the snake's head: further, the two halves of the lower jaw are not connected by bone but by ligaments.

A more serious objection is raised by Mr. Douglas St. L. Gordon in *Dartmoor in all its Moods* (pp. 274-5). He writes:—

'The difficulties of belief are numerous . . . , but most insuperable, perhaps, is the question of time. The act of swallowing even one young viper could scarcely be otherwise than a lengthy proceeding, and if the reptile can indeed absorb its entire family in the space of a few seconds, it must be a singularly gifted creature, particularly when one remembers that the adder is viviparous, its brood numbering as many as fifteen—a liberal mouthful.'

I have received a good many first-hand descriptions of the alleged swallowing from correspondents in Somerset and Devon. The most convincing came from Jim George, the Mendip woodman who married my old nurse. He was an intelligent man and his honesty was beyond question. He saw an adder lying curled up and approached her with a stone in his hand: to quote his own words 'there were a lot o' little young 'uns all crawling in and out o' the grass along by her, and their little eyes did shine. And she did open her mouth and they did all run in one after another'. He flung the stone and hit her, and 'cut her innards all out: and she did hiss at I that loud after I'd hit her, most as if it were a whistle: and I seed all those little young 'uns come out of her where the stone cut her open: and after she were dead one on 'em tried to go in at her mouth again.'

The last sentence is most important. By this time the adder was dead and he was quite near her: the attempt of one of the young to enter her mouth again can hardly have been an optical illusion. If the young persisted in their attempt to enter their mother's mouth after her death, the inference is that the instinct existed during her lifetime.

Some four or five years ago Mr. J. Hanks, of Plymouth, wrote a very vivid account in the *Western Morning News* of the occurrence at Bigbury, S. Devon, in August 1932. He turned over a canvas bag lying on a grassy slope, and found three adders beneath it. They remained still for a few seconds, then the middle one 'appeared to be raising its head and about three inches of its body slightly, and instantly a young one darted out from beneath it and came practically to my feet, turned, and danced back straight into the mouth of the middle one, followed by another and others at rather incredible speed. The head of one was close to the tail of the foregoing one. It was like a string of dancing black beads: every one followed exactly the route of the first, and the old one appeared, by working its jaws and the raised part of its body to help in the process. By the shape of the old one the position inside was visible from three to five inches from the head.' He estimated the number of young ones from nine to thirteen. The grass all around the bag had been eaten off quite close by rabbits, and the ground was bare under the bag.

When this account appeared I sent a short note to the paper recapitulating the present state of the evidence and received several letters on the subject. One was from a Williton correspondent, Mr. A. S. Rew:

'I have twice witnessed this event, but many years ago. The first instance was during my school-days, when proceeding home I saw an adder "basking" on a ledge in the hedge in front of an old rabbit burrow. I did not attempt to molest it but stood for a few seconds looking at at, when it suddenly raised its head slightly, made a peculiar grating hiss, which caused a scurry and rustle amongst the grass, etc., immediately surrounding her bed, and out popped five young ones. The five young ones, without any hesitation, wriggled to the front of her, wheeled in perfect order and rotation, darted for her open mouth, and disappeared down her throat so quickly that the whole event was over in about eight seconds.

'The second instance happened, curiously enough, within a quarter of a mile of the first. The adder was basking on the crown of a fairly low hedge. The same noise was uttered, the same movements executed by the young, this time four in number. The size of the young in each case was about the same, that is approximately three to three and a half inches long. The second event was witnessed about 1925 or 1926, the first about 1912.

'There is no question of the happening being an optical illusion. My first view was from the front, my second from the side-front, and in both cases I had a clear view of the ground or earth immediately behind the adder. I did not attempt to kill the adder.'

The similarity between the two accounts is obvious: they both stress the regularity of the movements of the young adders. Mr. Hanks' observation of the working of the old adder's jaw is of exceptional interest, for it is similar to the reptile's action when swallowing its prey. Some years ago I was walking with my wife along a shady lane—the last place where you would expect to find an adder on a hot day—and stepped over it without seeing it. My wife saw it and called out to me. It was stretched across the path, in the act of swallowing a fledgling. The bird's head and shoulders were already inside its gullet; the swelling caused by the skull was quite visible. But for the fact that its mouth was full, it might have struck at me as I stepped over it.

Seeing us, it disgorged its prey, and slithered off to the shelter of a hole in a wall. Examining the young bird more closely, we could observe the snake's *modus operandi*. The nestling's head and shoulders were covered with saliva, and drawn out from the rest of the body. The legs trailed behind; once the adder's gape was widened enough to admit the head, the rest would be easy. As I have explained above, the adder's mouth, skull and skeleton are ingeniously adapted to the swallowing process. Mr. Hanks' account suggests that the adder when swallowing its young acts in the same way as when it swallows its prey.

I have also before me two other circumstantial reports of an adder swallowing her young, which follow, *mutatis mutandis*, the accounts set out in detail above. In each instance the adder was violently killed: in once case the body was opened with a penknife and the young taken out alive and in the other they were squeezed out of the carcass and wriggled away. I have no doubt of the accuracy of these statements. But, as I have already mentioned, the adder's oviduct extends some two thirds of her length towards the head; a scientist would at once refuse to accept these instances as proof on the ground that, as the carcass had been violently treated, it is impossible to say definitely whether the young were in the gullet or in the oviduct. Reading the vivid statements of the eye witnesses in these cases, I am of a different opinion. But for the reasons given I do not quote these accounts in full.

That the adder swallows her young has not been scientifically proved: still less has it been disproved. I find it difficult to believe that all the recorded instances, some of them related by educated people, are illusions, optical or otherwise. I prefer to keep an open mind; and I have Gilbert White on my side. For, of the woodcock carrying its young, which he doubted, he wrote: 'But candour forbids me to say absolutely that any fact is false because I have never been witness to such a fact.'

Finally, I would ask anyone who sees—or thinks he sees—an adder swallow her young, to kill her as painlessly as possible (a smart blow with a stick where the head joins the body will cause instant death), tie a noose tightly round the neck and send the carcass to the keeper of the Zoological Department of the British Museum for expert examination.

You hear curious tales on Exmoor about bites of adders, and their remedies. An old woman was bitten one day on the leg. A friend visited the spot a few days after, at the hour when she had been bitten, and killed the adder. From its body he extracted an oil which, applied to the bitten place, effected a complete cure. Nevertheless the anniversary of the bite was always celebrated by a swelling on the lady's leg, which uncannily took an adder's shape.

One day in May I saw an adder crossing the road in Horner, near Porlock. The road was thick with dust and the reptile evidently found it difficult to get any purchase, for it made but slow progress

until it reached the herbage across the road. It left a track about two
inches broad, and in the middle was a sharp, wavy indentation such
as is seen in worm-tracks, probably caused by contractions of the
muscles. Marks of the segments of the snake's body were also visible.
As the creature crawled in the dust its forked tongue shot in and out:
surely here is the origin of 'dust shalt thou eat'.

CHAPTER XXI

MOORLAND PEACE

One February day I drove with friends in a car to Oare Post, Chetsford Bridge, Exford, Withypool, Winsford, Cutcombe, Timberscombe, Wootton Courtenay, Luccombe, and so home to Porlock. This journey shows you all that is most lovely on the eastern side of Exmoor. It was one of those clear, quiet, almost windless days when the peace of moorlands sinks into the mind.

As Dr. Vaughan Cornish, in *The Poetic Impression of Natural Scenery*, writes of the English landscape in February, ' . . . in such surroundings and on such days the soul is satisfied and at peace. . . .' The source of the day's happiness lies, he says, 'in those satisfactions of the visual sense which create an emotional state, and it is when viewed emotionally that scenery reveals its deepest beauty.'

Every country-lover can recall memories in which the 'emotional state' created is peaceful and satisfying. Things often rise suddenly and unaccountably to the surface from the sub-conscious mind: no doubt there is always some forgotten association with the preceding train of thought, but the clue is missing. I have in memory many such mental land and seascapes. One March day, as I walked down the hill called Bush Steep towards the Selworthy Woods, I was suddenly conscious of a vivid sense of the aliveness of Nature—the individual trees, the fields, the woods, the whole landscape, were pulsating with life and vigour. This sensation persisted during the rest of my walk, round Breakneck and across to Newbridge on the Minehead road. Bridges describes a similar experience in *The Testament of Beauty* :—

> To such a mood I had come, by what charm I know not,
> where on thatt upland path I was pacing alone;
> and yet was nothing new to me, only all was vivid
> and significant that had been dormant or dead.

I know that this intense aliveness in Nature is constant; it must have been my mood which made me realise its presence so strongly; and yet it was a raw, March day with a bitter north-west wind shrivelling a pinched landscape and snow still lying on the purple slopes of Dunkery. But the sensation imparted by the aliveness of the landscape was not unrestful, for nothing jarred upon the senses.

There is a canal somewhere in central France, with cool, green waters shadowed by poplars, towering breathless above it on a sultry

summer evening. Another memory is of the blanched whiteness of
Swiss snow mountains before dawn; their calm has the frozen, fixed
tranquillity of a dead man's eyes: it chills the blood, but its silent
beauty fascinates. Contrast with this the utter stillness of a pine
forest whose dim vistas exude a heavy resinous scent beneath the
unwinking rays of an August noon. Often there comes back to me
the azure calm of the sea on a summer's evening, on which clouds
cast shadows vague and immense as ideals dreamed but never attained. Beech woods, with splashes of fire on their fading foliage,
and a noiseless cloth of gold spread round their smooth, bare boles
embalm the spirit of autumn. The long, low lines of the Downs, with
their hollows sombred by yews, are restful to eye and brain.

To lean over the parapet of a bridge and gaze into watery depths
untroubled save by the sinuous waving of fishy tails can induce a
state of mind not far removed from the 'passivity' of quietists. All
scenes such as this bear witness to the power of Nature to 'impress'
the mind 'with quietness and beauty'. Their memory, recollected
in times of stress, recreates tranquillity.

But to me it is the peace of the moors which is most complete and
most satisfying. Here, as Plotinus says, 'Nature stands quietly at gaze
within herself.' To understand this peace you must know the moors
not only in summer when ling and heather clothe them splendidly,
but at all seasons. For moorland peace has infinite varieties, and each
kind makes its individual appeal. In spring the heather which clothes
the higher reaches is brown and dun, but lower down crockets of
sprouting fern and fragile bells of wild hyacinths spread a shimmering veil of delicate green and cærulean blue. Springtime peace is
joyful: there is a throb in it.

As summer broadens, bracken fronds become a six-foot forest of
miniature palms: around them there is a hum of myriad insect wings,
and aromatic drowsy scents which mingle with the nectar breath of
heather, and later of ling. Now there are moonlit nights when glow-
worms shine like fallen moonbeams, and all is silent but the far-off
spinning-wheel of a nightjar. On breathless July mornings the air is
so tranquil that distant voices can be heard a mile away. Summer
peace is sensuous.

In early autumn the heather flowering is over. Colour on the
moor has faded, though in the coombes birch and oak and rowan
and beech run riot in golds and browns of all shades. Dead grass
flashes yellow as sunlight strikes it and whortleberry leaves are blood
red. Bracken is tawny: soon rain and wind flatten its stalks, till it lies
tumbled and dishevelled like handfuls of rufous hair plucked from

the polls of giants. Autumn peace is tinged with the regret which clings to the evanescence of beauty.

There is no more desolate sight than a moorland landscape in winter under a snow-laden sky; purple shadows are reflected from the snow's crystals even upon the trunks of thorns, oaks and beeches. But in sunshine all is different. I remember, some thirty years ago, climbing Scaw Fell Pikes at Easter; we ascended through snow storms, but at the top the sun shone out; every one of the Lake hills was bathed in brilliance and seemed to beckon to us: northward we looked to the Cheviots, south to the smoke of Barrow-in-Furness and westward to highlands of the Isle of Man. So also from snow-clad Dunkery you may descry afar off Dartmoor's bastions shining white through haze, and a gleam may strike a patch of snow on the summit of Brecon Beacon.

Snow brings enchantment also to the wooded coombes which seam the moor. In their moist atmosphere every branch is in winter limned with grey lichen. Snow settles on these lichen-covered boughs: if it thaws and then freezes its weight may tear them from the trunks, leaving raw scars. But a light fall scarcely bends the twigs, and so transforms a grey fairyland into a white one. There are grottoes and labyrinths of shining filigree, through which, if frost has cleared the air, your eye travels to skies whose blue holds not the unfathomable hues of summer but that mild brilliance which belongs to winter. This snowy silence breathes peace.

But in winter it is after rain that moorland colouring is most subtle: then the hills mourn

In flowing purple for their lord forlorn,

but there are embroideries on their robes, of russet, of yellow, both pale and tawny, and of meagre brown, with here and there an inlay of vivid green from moss or bog-grass. Or there are the days when the moor is swathed in a dense, white vapour which pearls every heather twig, impenetrable to sight and full of strange unrecognisable sounds. Or again, sea-mist may come creeping in like a live creature, crouching in the valleys while slopes above are basking in sunshine. Even when gales are raging you can find quiet and shelter behind ten-foot beech-hedges, topping a bank, for throughout winter their withered leaves cling until in spring eager buds detach them. The moorland stretches before you league on league. Here, too, is winter peace.

Yet there is one moorland scene which, though peaceful, brings to me a sense of discomfort that is sometimes acute. Looking down from some slight eminence—a bank or tumulus—over a waste of heather and rough grass, your eye lights upon some distant and solitary pool of stagnant water. Such a prospect brings to me instantaneously a sense of melancholy. Though I have often probed my mind for the reason, it escapes me. The feeling indeed appears quite unreasonable. Probably it is due to some ancient association, buried deep and long forgotten. But others have told me that they experience the same sensation.

Dr. Vaughan Cornish, in the book I have already mentioned, remarks that our receptivity to the silent speech of Nature depends upon our moods, or even upon our physical condition—a true but humiliating fact. As Emerson very truly wrote, 'the difference between landscape and landscape is small, but there is a great difference in the beholders.'

Why is it that moorland peace is the deepest? I think it is because on the moors we are nearest to Earth's face. In typical moorland country there are few trees, except perhaps a stunted thorn or blasted rowan. Only heather or ling, and the peat which their decay has formed through immemorial generations, separates us from primeval rocks, the very bones of Earth, our Mother. But for this thin covering the hills lie as they did when the waters receded. Also, there is silence save for the scrannel pipe of wind in the heath; curlew's skirl or raven's croak only intensify the succeeding stillness. Lie prone upon moorland heather and you can hear Earth's heart beating.

RETURN

When I am dead, if aught survives of me
　　'Twill be a core of spirit, purged of sin,
　　A tiny, flickering tongue of flame within
The throbbing pulses of eternity ;
No more confined in irksome flesh, but free
　　To follow Beauty's star, perchance to win
　　Her Holy of Holies, there to enter in—
Enough were this of Immortality.

And if, so purged, the spirit be still aware,
　　—Drawn by compulsive urge of memory—
　　Of earthly scenes once hallowed by its love,
I shall return, like a small wayward air,
　　O'er heath and ling and brownèd fern to rove,
And home in some deep goyal on Dunkery.

INDEX

ADDER, 22, 32, 148–53
  ash charm of, 48
  bones, structure of, 149, 152
  cannibalism? 149
  Exmoor superstition as to, 48, 152
  oviduct, 148, 152
  swallowing prey, 151–2
  swallowing young? 148–53
  track of, 153
  young, number of, 150, 151
Aeschylus, death of, 86
Albinism, stoat, 21
Alfoxton Park, 117–20
Anecdotes, West Country, 49
Ants, and slow-worms, 22–3
Armstrong, E. A., *Bird Display*, 66
Ash, medicinal and magic qualities, 48
Ashen faggot, 47, 48
Autumn song, 144–7

Badger, 27–8, 32
Bagley Combe, 47
Barley, 125
Batten, H. Mortimer, *The Badger Afield and Underground*, 28
Beebe, W., *Nonsuch, Land of Water*, 97
Beech, 117–18, 155
Bergson, *Duration*, 91
Berners, Juliana, 112
Bewick, *History of British Birds*, 94
Bicknoller Combe, 118
Birch, 14, 19, 111
Bird-bath, 16–17
BIRDS
  aesthetic approach to, 98, 145
  autumn song, 144–7
  behaviour, 57, 65, 66, 84
  breeding cycle, 65–6
  caged, 67, 141
  can they count? 89–91
  individuality in, 63–4, 74, 92–3
  inherited memory, 98
  injured, 18, 19, 97–8, 140–1
  instinct and intelligence, 67, 86–9

life history of, 63–4
looking in the face, 15–16
mating, meaning of, 94
nestlings and thirst, 88
pairing for life, 93–4
protection, 140, 142
psychology, 43
ringing, 61, 63, 64–6, 72, 93–4, 100–8.
routine and, 84–6
sanctuaries, 140
St. Francis and, 139, 142
tables, 15, 140
time, sense of, 91
wastage in, 61, 97
BLACKBIRD, 93, 109
  age, 103
  cock brooding, 102
  injured, survival of, 97
  merlin's prey, 31
  musical phrases in song, 102–3, 108
  ringing, 101–3
  solitary, 93, 113
  song, 102–3, 110, 112–13, 144, 145
  tame, 102
  territory, 93, 103, 113
  unintelligence, 86
Blackcap, 15, 111, 145
BLACKCOCK, 121–4
  display, 121–3
  grey hens, 121, 123
  'heath poults', 121
  lekking places, 121–3
  notes, 122–3
  plumage, 122
'Bluebells', 124
Bond, Miss P., *Watching Wild Life*, 84
Brambling, 53, 62, 129
Bratton Court, 46
Bridges, Robert, 75, 115, 154
British Bird Book, The, 96
Brooks-King, M., (note), 56
'Buckland', 49
Bullfinch, in snow, 112

Bunting, cirl, 14, 16, 59
  routine behaviour, 85
  song, 132, 144
  unintelligence, 86–7
Bunting, corn, 58
Bunting, reed, 126
Bunting, snow, 126
Bunting, yellow, *see* Yellow-hammer
Burkitt, J. P., 107
Buzzard, 32, 34, 92, 98, 110, 119
  threatening humans, 92

Cat, homing instinct, 28
CHAFFINCH, 15, 16, 51–75, 129, 140
  age, 64, 67, 73
  altitude, 52, 53
  bathing habits, 61–2
  call-notes, 55, 56–7, 69, 71
  coition, 57, 68
  Continental, 63
  courage, 59
  courtship and display, 57–8, 69
  distribution, 52, 64
  eggs, 60, 61, 65, 68–71
  fledging period, 61, 69, 71
  flocks, 53, 129
  flocks, proportion of sexes in, 52–3
  food, 61, 62, 70
  gait, 62–3
  'Gouty', 59, 64, 68–73
  hens, visits to old nesting sites, 60
  song of, 54–5
  incubation, 60, 61, 68–9, 72, 73
  injured, recovery of, 59, 64, 97
  intelligence, 59–60, 73
  mating fidelity, 65, 93–4, 108
  mentality, 59, 60
  migration, 63
  nests, 'decorated', 60
  nesting, 60–1, 64, 65, 68–73
  nest sanitation, 61, 70
  plumage, 51–2, 62, 63
  posturing while feeding young, 65–6, 72
  prey of merlin, 31, 53
  pugnacity, 57, 59, 60, 65
  ringing, 63, 64–6, 72, 93
  roosting, 63
  routine behaviour, 84–5
  song, 53–6, 60, 145

dialects, 55–6
  effect on weather on, 54
  hen, of, 54–5
  period, 53–4, 56, 60
  phrases of, 54
  verbal renderings, 56
  young, of, 56
  tameness, 59, 62, 64, 67–75, 84-5
    (*and see* 'Gouty')
  territorial sense, 60, 64, 72–3
  trapping, 64
  unintelligence, 59–60, 86
  young, 61–2, 67
  young mortality, 61
  young fed by hen only, 69, 71
  'William the Silent', 74
Chadwyck-Healey, Sir C., *History of Part of West Somerset*, 45
Chalk Water, 110
Chiff-Chaff, 145
Cherry, 113
Clarke, Dr. Eagle, *Studies in Bird Migration*, 37, 145
Coleridge, S. T., 119, 137
Collectors, 135
Collett, A., *The Heart of a Bird*, 52–3
Coot, 142
Cornwall Bird-Watching, etc., Society, 37
Cornish, A. V., 133–4
Cothelstone Beacon, 119
Country dress, former, 76–7
COURSER, CREAM COLOURED, 133–4
  crouching, 134
  flight, 133
  legs, colour of, 134
  notes, 133
  peregrine and, 134
  plumage, 133–4
  posture, 134
Coward, T. A., 38, 135
Crab apples, 113
Crow, carrion, 32, 86, 90, 111, 124
Crow, grey, can count, 90
Cuckoo, 124
  'Hibernation' of, 94–5
  prey of merlin, 30
Culpeper, *Complete Herbal*, 48
Cupressus macrocarpa, 14
Curlew, 111, 128, 129, 157

Delamain, J., 41
  Why Birds sing, 139, 146
Devon Bird-Watching, etc., Society, 37
'Didley Dab', 49
Dillies, 80
'Dinderduck', 49
Dipper, 93, 109, 119
  song, 144
Dormouse, 27
Dorrien-Smith, Major, 42
'Drapier's pence', 14
Duck, long-tailed, 128
Duck, tufted, 128, 142
'Dulverton men', 128
Dunlin, 126
DUNNOCK, 18
  age, 103–4, 108
  hen singing, 104
  nesting, 103–4
  pairing for life, 104
  ringing, 103–4
  robin's hostility to, 15, 92
  song, winter, 144
  toad in nest of, 23

Eeles, Dr. F. C., 44
Emerson, 157
'Emotional state', 154
Exmoor, 13, 20, 46, 50, 52, 92, 93,
  109, 114, 117, 118, 119, 121,
  144, 152, 154

Falconer, D. S. (note), 56
Fieldfare, 98
Field-mouse, long-tailed, 20
Flycatcher, spotted, 17–18
  nesting, 17–18
  sanitation of young out of nest, 86
Fox, 27, 32, 110, 118, 119
Frog, medicinal quality of, 48–9

Galsworthy, Life and Letters of, 141
  Forsytes, Pendyces and Others, 98
Garnett, E., 98
George, James and Emma, 76–83, 150
Gibbard, S. D., 55
Gilbert and Brook, *Watchings and Wan-
  derings Among Birds*, 88
Gladstone, Sir H., 123
Goldcrest, 59

injured, 19
Goldfinch, 19, 53, 63, 93, 111, 120
  merlin's prey, 32
Goldfinches and Cherry Blossom, 115–16
Goose, brent, 128
Goose, grey-lag, 128
Goose, white-fronted, 128
Gordon, Seton, *Thirty Years of Nature
  Photography*, 90–1
Gordon, D. St. L., *Dartmoor in all its
  Moods*, 149–50
GOUTY, 59, 64, 68–73
Grebe, great crested, 92
Greenfinch, 15, 16, 52, 53, 92
  age, 100
  merlin's prey, 34
  ringing, 100
  shyness, 100
Greenshank, 127
Grey, Lord, *The Charm of Birds*, 51, 54,
  55, 145–7
Grouse, black, *see* Blackcock
Grouse, red, 35, 121
Gulls, 110, 129
Gull, black-headed, 85, 129
Gull, common, 85, 129
Gull, herring, 85, 86, 129
Gull, greater black-backed, 129

'Hallelujah Field', 49
Handbook of British Birds, 57, 99, 134
Hanks, J., 150, 151, 152
Hare, 20
Harrier, Hen, 31
Heather, 112, 117, 155
Hedgehog, 24, 32
Hegel, 63
Heron, 32, 128
Hibernation,
  cuckoo, 94–5
  squirrel, 25
Hoatzin, 98
Howard, Eliot, 60, 84
Hudson, W. H., 98, 137
Hurdle and 'spick' making, 77–81
Huxley, Julian, *Bird Watching and Bird
  Behaviour*, 146

Ingram and Salmon, *Birds in Britain
  Today*, 61, 98

L

Jackdaw, 114
  survival of injured, 97
Jay, 18, 97, 112, 124
  mimicry, 137–8
  song, 137–8
Junco, 146

Kearton, J., 88
Kennet, Lord, *A Bird in the Bush*, 142
Kestrel, 59, 98, 118
  killing blue tit, 17
  depriving thrush of worm, 104
  roosting in gargoyle, 109
Kilve, 120
Kingfisher, 109, 128
Knot, 126

Lack, D. (note) 56
  The Life of the Robin (note), 108
Lapwing, 93
Lark, shore, 128
Lark, sky, 145
  altitude, 37
  merlin's prey, 35
Lark, white-winged, 135
Lark, wood, 14–15, 113, 144, 146
Linnet, 53, 129
Ligue Française pour la Protection des Oiseaux, 140
Lister, M. D. (note), 56
Little Flowers of St. Francis, The, 139
Lizard, 23
Luccombe Church, 109
Luttrell, G. F., 134

Magpie, 70, 97, 124
  killing slow-worm, 23
Mallard, 141
'Mare Meadow', 50
'Marlands', 50
Marples, G. and A., *Sea Terns or Sea Swallows*, 90–1
Marsden, Major W. M., 146
Martin, house, 120, 126
Martin, sand, 120, 126
Meredith, George, 61
MERLIN, 29–36, 129
  carrying young, 35
  courage, 32, 34
  courtship, 35

feigning injury? 33
  incubation, 30, 32
    by cock, 29, 34
  harmless to game, 35–6
  nesting, 29–35
  notes, 31, 35
  passing prey to young, 30
    cock to hen, 31, 34
  prey, 30–2, 34–5, 53, 129
  slaughter of, 35–6
  tree-nesting, protective, 32–3, 34, 35
  young, 29–32, 34
Migration, individualism in, 43
MIGRATION, SWALLOW, 37–43
  air currents, 37–8
  Bristol Channel, etc., 39, 40, 120, 126
  Brittany, from, 42
  Channel Islands, from, 42
  Cornwall, S. coast, 41, 42
  Dart, 41
  Dartmoor, over, 40, 41
  Devon, S. coast, 41, 42
  Dorset, S. coast, 42
  duration, 38, 39
  earlier in S.W. than in France, 42
  Eddystone, 41
  Erme, 40, 41
  Exe, 40–3
  Exmoor, over, 40
  Fal, 41
  France, W. and S.W., 38, 41–2
  home-coming, 43
  Ireland, 39
  Lundy Is., 39, 40
  Otter, 41
  Plymouth Sound, 41
  Quantocks, on, 120
  sea, arrivals over, 41, 42
  Sid, 41
  St. Erth, 41
  Tamar, 41
  Taw and Torridge, 39, 40
  Teign, 40
  Wales, S. and W., 39, 40
  weather conditions, 37–8
    turned back by, 42–3
  West Coast Route, 38–41
  Yealm, 40, 41
Moth, Emperor, 31

'Mother Uglies', 14
Munthe, Dr. A., *The Story of San Michele*, 139–40
Musk, sweet-smelling, 77

National Trust, 50
Nesting boxes, 17–18, 140
Nightingale
    bathing, 17
    singing in winter haunt, 146
Nightjar, 126, 132
Nuthatch, 17, 93, 111
    intelligence, 87–8
    routine behaviour, 85
    unintelligence, 85, 86, 88

Orchis, Early Purple, 14
Ornithology, intensive methods, 63, 98–9, 108
    scientific, 63, 135
Owl, little, 97
Owl, tawny, 67
Oyster-catcher, 128–9
    Gaelic legend as to, 129

Pan in the tree-tops, 26
Parham, H. J., *A Nature Lover in British Columbia*, 140
Partridge, 98
Peacock butterfly, 115
Peregrine, 119, 129, 134
    reversing, 130
    cream coloured courser, and, 134
Perry, R., *Lundy, Isle of Puffins*, 39
Phalarope, grey, 128
Philipson, W. R., 107
Pike, O., 88
Pipit, meadow, 31, 33, 124
    merlin's prey, 35, 129
Pitt, Miss Frances, 123, 127
    The Naturalist on the Prowl, 90
Place-names, local, 49–50
Plotinus, 155
Plover, golden, flocks, 93
Plover, green, *see* Lapwing
Plover, ringed, 126
Polecat, 21
Poplar, white, 110
Porlock, 44–50
    Church, 44–5

isolation, former, 45
local rhymes, 48–50
local stories, 46–8
local place-names, 49–50
smuggling, 45–6
Porlock Marsh, 50, 125–9
Pycraft, W. P., 95–6

Quantocks, 117–120

Rabbit, 20, 81, 121
    traps, 97–8
Rail, water, 98
Rat, eating trout, 20
RAVEN, 32, 33, 34, 35, 90, 109, 115, 119, 129, 130, 157
    bringing water to nestlings, 88
    nesting in trees, 136–7
    'unkindness' of, 112
    notes, 136
    sites of nests, 137
Ray, *Willughby's Ornithology*, 94
Red Admiral, 115
Red Deer, 110, 119, 129
Red Road, the, 114–15
Redshank, 120, 126, 127
Redstart, black, 18–19
Redstart, common, 111
Renier, J. G., *A Tale of Two Robins*, 89–90
Rew, A. S., 151
Richmond, W. B., *England's Birds*, 43, 51, 109
    Quest for Birds, 98
Ringing, *see* 'Birds, ringing'
Ring Ousel, 110, 123
ROBIN, 15, 16, 67, 93, 104–8
    age, 107
    autumn song, 144–6
    can count? 89–90
    disappearance, 107
    hostility to dunnock, 15, 91
        to chaffinch, 59
    food, 89, 105
    matrimonial tangles, 106–7
    migration, 107–8
    mortality, 107
    nesting, 106
    posturing, 108
    ringing, 104–7

ROBIN, tame, 89, 92, 104–7
   territory, 93, 146
   toad in nest of, 23
Rook, 60, 86, 88, 114
Rowan, Professor, 146
Ruff, 127
Ruston, A. H., 75
Ryves, Col. and Mrs., 58

Sandpiper, Common, 126, 127
Sandpiper, Green, 127
Sanitation of nest, chaffinch, 61
   spotted flycatcher, 86
Saunders, Howard, 134
Scilly, Is. of, 38, 41, 42
Seigne, J. W., *A Birdwatcher's Notebook*, 35
Selous, E., 84, 123
   Realities of Bird Life, 66, 84
Selworthy Beacon, 50
Sheld-duck, 97, 120
Shoveler, 128
Shrike, red-backed, 35, 126
   larders, 126–7
Siskin, 15, 59, 135
Slow-worm, 22
   and ants, 22–3
   shamming death, 23
   killed by magpie, 23
Smuggling, 45–6
Snake, grass, 22, 126
Snipe, common, 129
   position of eye and ear, 96
Snipe, jack, 129
Snow, 71, 111–12, 115, 156
   in May, 111
Snow mountains, 155
SONG, BIRD (*see under* 'Birds' and various species)
   autumn, 144–7
   daylight and, 146
   meaning of, 145–7
   territory, and, 145, 146
   weather and, 146
   winter quarters, in, 146
Sparrow-hawk, 64, 98, 101
Spick or spar-making, 77–81
Sparrow, hedge, *see* Dunnock
Sparrow, house, 15, 19, 52, 53, 67, 92
Sparrow, tree, 53

Squirrel, grey, 26–7
Squirrel, red, 24–6
   anger, 25
   somnolence, 25
   Pan in the tree-tops, 26
Starling, 15, 59, 87, 92, 128, 135, 144
   bathing habits, 16–17
St. Francis of Assisi, 139, 142
Stint, little, 126
St. James's Park, waterfowl in, 141–2
Stonechat, 93, 112, 118, 129
Stoat, 20–1, 32, 97, 144
   local name, 22
Stork, bringing water to nestlings, 88
Sunrise, 114
Superstitions, 48–9, 152
Swainson, *The Folklore and Provincial Names of British Birds*, 56
Swallow migration, *see* Migration, swallow
Swallow, transport by aeroplane, 140

Teal, 126, 127–8
Tern, little, can count? 90–1
Terrier, 'Brandy', 21–2
Territory, 146
   blackbird, 93, 103
   chaffinch, 60, 72–3
   robin, 93
Thirst, nestlings and, 88–9
Thomson, Dr. A. Landsborough, *Problems of Bird Migration*, 146
Thomson, H. A. R., 55
Thompson, Ian M., *Birds from the Hide*, 92
Thrush, mistle, 59, 110, 144
   drinking, 17
Thrush, song, 15, 16, 59, 111, 144, 145
   age, 104
   counting? 89–90
   deprived of worm by kestrel, 104
   nesting first year, 104, 108
   not hardy, 104
   ringing, 104
   stupid, 92
Tit, bearded, 92
TIT, BLUE, 15, 16, 17, 19, 59
   age, 100, 108
   bigamy, attempted, 101
   fledging period, 101

Tit, killed by kestrel, 17
  nesting, 17, 100–1
  marital affairs, 100–1
  pairing for life, 94, 108
  ringing, 100–1
Tit, cole, 15, 93
Tit, great, 15, 60, 86, 88, 93, 144
Tit, long-tailed, 18, 60, 93
Tit, marsh, 15, 93
Toad, 23–4
  climbing powers of, 23
  in birds and other nests, 23
  tame, 24
  'teasy', 49
  medicinal qualities, 48–9
  musical, 24

Underhill, Evelyn, Immanence, 142–3

Vaughan, Cornish, Dr., Poetic Impression
  of Natural Scenery, 109, 154, 157
Vole, 20, 23

Wagtail, blue-headed, 138
Wagtail, grey, 18, 119
  moistening food for young, 88
Wagtail, pied, 15, 62, 93
  migration, 120
Wagtail, white, 126, 127
Wagtail, yellow, 120, 126, 127, 138
Warbler, aquatic, 135
Warbler, garden, 145
Warbler, grasshopper, 132
Warbler, marsh, 126
Warbler, sedge, 126
Warbler, willow, 16, 145, 146
Warbler, wood, 145
Water, brought to nestlings, 88–9
Weasel, 20, 21, 97

local name for, 22
Weir Water, 110
Wheatear, 17, 120, 125–6
  merlin's prey, 35
Whimbrel, 120, 128
Whinchat, 118, 123
  merlin's prey, 34, 35
Whitethroat, common, 15
White, Gilbert, Natural History of Sel-
  borne, 52, 148, 152
Whymper, C., 95, 97
Wigeon, 128, 141
Willughby, Ornithology, 94
Woodcock, 135, 152
  ear, position of, 95–7
  eye, position of, 96
Woodlark, see Lark, wood
Woodpecker, black, 134–5
Woodpecker, greater spotted, 94
Woodpecker, green, 119, 144
WOODPECKER, LESSER SPOTTED, 130–3
  drumming, 131–3, 144
    vocal theory, 132–3
  feeding, 130–1
  intelligence, 88
  plumage, protective, 131
  routine behaviour, 85
Wood-pigeon, 111, 144
'Wood's Halfpence', 14
Words, 115
Wordsworth, Dorothy, 14, 119–20
Wordsworth, William, 14, 119–20,
  138
Wren, 73, 93, 144–6
  bathing habits, 16

Yellow-hammer, 53
  toad in nest of, 23
Yule Log, 47–8